For Jim -

with love at

Judith

15 October 2018

THINKING ABOUT SNOW

THINKING ABOUT SNOW

JUDITH McCLURE

Maclean Dubois

This edition first published in hardback in Great Britain
in 2018 by Maclean Dubois
14/2 Gloucester Place, Edinburgh EH3 6EF

ISBN: 978 0 9565278 7 5

British Library Cataloguing-in-Publication Data
A catalogue record for this book is available on request
from the British Library.

Designed and typeset in Garamond by Abigail Salvesen.
Printed and bound by Gutenberg Press, Malta.

For Roger: thinking together for forty years plus

ACKNOWLEDGEMENT

Heartfelt thanks to the great and generous novelist Alexander McCall Smith, to the incomparable editorial team of Lesley Winton, copy editor Nicola Wood and designer Abigail Salvesen, to my great friend Clare Hayes, to the Education Department of Middlesbrough Council, who gave incredible support to my education from 1950–1973, to my old friends from the Newlands Grammar School and to Matthew Naylor, Archive and Heritage Centre Co-Ordinator, Institute of Our Lady of Mercy GB.

FOREWORD

Judith McClure is known to many in Scotland and indeed in the wider world as an innovative and outward-looking educationalist. But what many people do not know – and this applies to her countless friends in all walks of life – is that she spent a number of years as a nun. How she came to do that, and what happened to her in those years, is the subject of this beautiful memoir.

What emerges from reading of this book is, I think, a sense of Judith's intensely engaging personality. This is a story of a spiritual journey, but it is also an account of how such a journey takes place in a social and political context. In particular, it provides a critique of authority and the role that authority may seek to play in religious life. Judith opts for freedom, but she does not do so in any selfish, self-indulgent way: she sees freedom as a necessary prerequisite of both the intellectual and the spiritual life.

This is not a long book. It may be read in one sitting, and at the end the reader has a feeling of having spent a couple of hours in the company of an exceptionally sympathetic and perspicacious mind. For those of us who are fortunate enough to call Judith McClure our friend, there is the additional satisfaction of revelation. Now we can articulate, with greater understanding, just what it is that makes her one of the most exceptional and interesting women of her generation.

Alexander McCall Smith

THINKING ABOUT SNOW

1

On a sunny day in July 1970, my friend Clare and I travelled from Westgate-on-Sea to London by the first train. We had left the Convent of the Canonesses of St Augustine for the last time; I had ceased to be a nun after six years, Clare after five.

My mood in crowded London was euphoric: it was wonderful to have left the enclosed world, to feel the pavement under my feet, and to know I was not wearing a veil. We decided to have breakfast at a place that for us symbolised freedom, choice and self-indulgence: the Lyons Strand Corner House. It had to be The Full English. I shall never forget the sight of that glorious plate of fried eggs, sausages, bacon, mushrooms, tomato, baked beans and perfect toast. I was left with four old pence in my pocket to begin the rest of my life, aged twenty-four, but the sense of freedom set material concerns at naught.

The next train took us to Oxford, where Clare and I moved into a flat at 300 Woodstock Road. She was about to start a primary teaching post and I to begin a degree in history at Somerville College. Our landlady was Mrs Elisabeth Newcombe, who was in her seventies and confined to a wheelchair. But she believed life was to be lived to the full. A French woman, she had married Lieutenant-Colonel Stuart Newcombe, a former commanding officer of Lawrence of

Arabia. She told us how, as a young woman during the First World War, she had rescued her husband from a Turkish prison camp, dressed as a washerwoman and carrying women's clothes for his escape in her bundle.

It was a propitious and lively start to my university career. Clare and I unpacked our trunks. There was not much physical baggage: for six years, since the age of eighteen, I had lived a communal life, stripped of personal possessions, with essential items from handkerchiefs to my religious habit marked simply with my number: 37. Opening up my luggage, however, brought home the immense contrast between the pared-down physical remnants of those years in an enclosed order, and their intense intellectual and emotional content.

At first sight the items seemed innocuous enough: I was wearing my only ordinary set of clothes, the dated and lifeless grey suit I had worn when I entered the convent. There was a bible, heavily annotated in pencil, and there were well-worn towels and a toothbrush. But there were also the hard-backed A5 notebooks in which I had written my thoughts during many retreats, and the 'discipline': the small whip of knotted cords used for self-flagellation. I kept the bible, but it did not take me long to decide what to do with the rest. Although I was to read history, and the past and its influence were forever in my mind, I threw everything into the dustbin. I could not bear to preserve my words, because I believed that for the last six years as a nun, I had surrendered my mind. One day, I thought, I would write about that experience and how it came about.

Since then, I have imagined my life as a single year, moving relentlessly on and characterised by changing seasons. I was born at the winter solstice, so on my accounting I am unlikely to see another. Now, in my early seventies, I am in the first week of October. It is a time to anticipate the delights of full autumn, unmarred yet by the dark winter to come. I find I want to reflect on the cold, brisk months of January and February, when I found my being and upon which all my thoughts are founded, and the March of my life as a nun.

My first memory is that of being dragged from sleep by the piercing wail of an air raid siren. I am lying curled up in bed in the dark and I know that I am helpless. I am very young and I have not learned to talk. After a few terrifying minutes of the shocking sound, the shape of my mother appears by the bed. She is wearing her chocolate-brown coat with a fur collar and somehow I know she is going to carry me to the air raid shelter in the garden. The horror of the siren and the swift saving arms of my mother have constantly recurred in my mind, but of the shelter and the air raid there is nothing. The memory of this dream was strong in the early years of my childhood, and it took some time for me to realise that I had been born in December 1945, after the end of the Second World War.

The dream must have been the product of the active imaginings of a young child, hearing unnoticed the talk of parents and grandparents, uncles, aunts and their friends. For although I belong to the post-war generation, my life was bound up with the impact of the two World Wars of the twentieth century, which shaped the development of my mind, my ideas and my attitude to adult life.

My grandfather on my mother's side fought in the Royal Garrison Artillery at the Battle of the Somme in 1916. He returned to his family, with a tiny French Missal abandoned in the field, and to the silent contemplation of his experiences, about which he never spoke, and to what I heard was an unhappy relationship with his wife. Later in my childhood I read of the horrors that the men who fought on the Somme and in other battles of the First World War suffered, and the agonising injuries and deaths that they witnessed. I saw the powerful, grainy films of their going over the top, into a hell of bursting shells and gunfire. I was amazed by their courage and endurance.

My father, Jim, was in a reserved occupation in the Second World War. He was a police officer in Middlesbrough, and his was the task of preserving order in those dark, austere days, preventing black market dealings, seeking out enemy aliens, enforcing the black-out and stopping the dispersal of firearms, as well dealing with crime and supporting the dignity and hope of the community. His brother, my uncle Harry, fought in the Far East and was a prisoner-of-war; he returned bowed, the visible reminder of the unspoken sufferings he had endured.

My mother, Vera, had lived through both the wars. She saw the inwardness of her father, returning to manage a Co-op in Hartlepool, and its impact on the life of the family in their little end-terrace house in Burn Valley Road. As a young mother of my two elder brothers, Jimmy and David, she lived through the anxious and difficult days of the Second World War in Middlesbrough. For her, the answer was a life of steady dedication to the needs of others and not to herself, of steadfast faith and the resilience to support her family and friends whatever the circumstances.

My second early memory is more secure, though unclear in time. I think it took place before I started school. I am standing in the living room of 75 Southwell Road, staring out into the blizzard masking the back garden. Nothing can be seen of the three lilac trees at the end of the tiny patch of grass, nor of the even closer laburnum marking the spot at which my mother would chat to her friend and neighbour over the fence. So I focus on the snowflakes and I am amazed to see first of all that they are cream and even yellow, not white. Then I look at individual flakes and see that they are not coming straight down to earth, or even driven by the wind in one direction, though that is what appears. They move fast, but in all directions. I realise suddenly that this is what thinking must mean. There are things in my head that nobody knows about unless I choose to tell them. I am exhilarated by the sense of the independent actions of my own mind, now considering a humble subject but capable of so much, by its own force alone. This sense of excitement at the power of thought and the independent life of the individual mind has never left me.

So I remember my childhood most as a joyful search for knowledge and meaning, safe in a small home and the focus of loving parents. As a detective sergeant in the Middlesbrough CID, my father worked shifts and wore plain clothes: I never saw him in uniform. His father, Samuel McClure, had been born in Belfast but moved as a child to Hartlepool. He had travelled to Boston, then back to Hartlepool to work in the shipyards. There Jim had met my mother, who was working in a baker's shop, on an evening walk in an area known at the time as 'the hen run'. Both had left school at fourteen. He was a Roman Catholic and they married in church, she willingly promising to bring up any children in the same religion.

The 1930s cannot have been an easy time to set up a family. For my father, it meant that his whole life was to be dedicated to supporting my mother and their three children, my two elder brothers and me. He obtained a mortgage to purchase the house where I thought about snow in Middlesbrough, a three-bedroom semi-detached new build, for £600, and this was the centre of the family's existence. For my mother, her life was supporting him and bringing up Jimmy, David and me. She was not a dedicated housewife or a natural cook, but she was a wholly committed mother and she undertook the practical labours of running the household as the necessary accompaniment.

I lived at 75 Southwell Road for the first eighteen years of my life, from the winter solstice to the end of February in my reckoning. The imagery of winter is harsh and cruel but in fact life was solid and warm. As a child I was aware of rationing but food was plentiful; I had no reason to expect or want a range of choices. Sunday's joint served for the week in various forms, as did the cake baked that day. Butter, cut from a barrel-shaped block, was not spread thickly, and cheese and jam were served economically. Vera shopped regularly and carefully, going to 'the top', mysteriously the main road to the right, or 'the bottom', at the end of Southwell Road. Before I went to school I would go with her, watching her careful progression from shop to shop and her husbanding of her resources. My father gave her cash each week to spend on food and clothes; I remember at one stage it was £7. There was no accounting of how she spent it, which made visiting the Co-op at 'the top' and filling in the coupons which would result in a small dividend, 'the divvy', all the more important when she wanted to buy larger items.

Vera was thirty-eight when I was born and her life was clear and well established. My brothers were thirteen and eight years older than I respectively and I was, as the only daughter, very cherished. My elder brother described me late in his life as 'spoilt rotten'! For some reason Vera did not expect that I would help her in the house; she would prepare meals and wash them up, leaving me free to play in the garden and in the road, and above all to read. It was not an intellectual household: my father had his police textbooks, *The Daily Express* was delivered each day, and my mother received women's magazines. My brothers had their comics, especially the *Beano* and *The Eagle*, and I enjoyed these. I had a great zeal for finding out about the world and literary snobbery was unknown to me: I read whatever came to hand and sought out what I could.

A great find, in the early days, was *The New Book of Knowledge*, bought by my father, whose ten volumes, beginning with A–Beth, were illustrated with black and white pictures and photographs. My first serious interest in history came from puzzling over a picture of Hitler surrounded by banners, and wondering why he was given the respectful title of *Herr* Hitler. Eventually I worked out that that edition of *The New Book of Knowledge* had been published in 1934, and had my first lesson in the proper understanding of the dating of evidence. To supplement this were the public libraries: I still remember the delight of eventual admission to the adult library with its reference section. There was even the occasional purchase, pocket money saved, from Middlesbrough's only bookshop, Boddy's. My copy of Lancelot Hogben's *Science for the Citizen* was a great support in my first encounters with specialist science in early secondary school and was supplemented by the excellent Teach Yourself series. I fancied I would become a nuclear physicist when I was aged eleven, and filled notebooks with drawings of reactors and tried ignorantly to solve chemical equations.

It was a matter of using the resources to hand, in the pursuit of knowledge. These included Middlesbrough itself, its streets, its museum, its park and its Transporter Bridge. Albert Park was gracious and lined with trees and flower-beds; it had tennis courts and a lake with rowing boats (for a penny) and motor boats (for sixpence), which could be navigated around three tiny islands. There was a playground, with swings and roundabouts and no attendants. It was taken for granted that I could go anywhere, as I wished. The only advice I received was never to go with strangers, and always to avoid men in macs who hovered where children were playing. I never encountered either variety of threat but was glad of the sensible words.

At the main entrance of the park were the war memorial, and tablets with the names of all the citizens who had died in the two World Wars. These again brought home the nature of the past of my immediate family, while the nearby Dorman Museum and the statues of Bolckow and Vaughan, great iron masters, recalled Middlesbrough's rise to industrial size and importance in the nineteenth century. Knowing my place in time and my town roots exhilarated me; I loved crossing the Transporter Bridge by the terrifying ladders and path over the top (thruppence).

I was conscious of my limited Middlesbrough experience. My world was bounded by my family and local friends, but most particularly by religion. From my earliest days the highlight of the week was attending Mass at the Church of St Philomena every Sunday morning. We always went at 11 o'clock, which allowed for a comfortable start to the day, but was regarded by some as rather soft.

The journey to St Philomena's was short: a mere ten minutes' walk to the end of Southwell Road, and thence along Park Road South. On the way we passed the synagogue, whereof I knew nothing and could get no answers, and the Scandinavian Seamen's Mission. Across from the Church of St Philomena was what we called generically the Protestant Church of St Barnabas. It was not customary to set foot in a Protestant church, except for the marriage of close relatives who were not Catholics. I remember my mother explaining to me that they were very ordinary inside, and that she had known immediately when she entered one that God was not present.

Catholicism was a minority denomination in Middlesbrough, but a tenacious one; in the 1950s it was strongly Irish in habit and in people. While my father was what was called a 'cradle Catholic', my mother had converted from a not-very-strong non-conformity in the year of my birth. She always retained an aversion to alcohol from her Primitive Methodist upbringing. My father was meticulous in the practice of his faith, but regarded it as a private matter, not to be discussed even with wife and family. He would never have missed Mass on Sunday and he led the family in saying the Rosary together whenever he was not working the night shift. The practice was much encouraged by the then Pope Pius XII, and there was a Rosary campaign in Middlesbrough itself, when the preacher spoke to an enthusiastic audience at the football ground: 'The family that prays together, stays together.'

My mother was a devout convert for whom the accretions that Catholicism had acquired over the centuries, and particularly in an Irish parochial context, were just as important as the fundamental tenets. She saw her religion as the only true one that could lead to a personal relationship with God. When she was receiving instruction, she smelled roses; when she asked the priest where they were, she was told there were none. She took this as a blessing from St Teresa of Lisieux, recognised for her support of converts, and it gave her a great sense of faith. On the dressing table in my parents' bedroom was a plaster statue of St Teresa, holding a bouquet of roses, accompanied by an entirely white figure of the Virgin Mary, the Immaculate Conception; the Sacred Heart, a figure of Jesus in a red robe smiling serenely and pointing to his heart, stood in the living room, on the mantelpiece. Vera went in and out of church on All Souls Day, 2 November, to repeat prayers and save a series of souls in Purgatory; the practice of religion was for her the basis of daily life and a constant matter of discussion with me.

Play at home was fortified by the annual generous load of birthday and Christmas gifts, which I piled on our well-used tea trolley and gloated over before consigning them to use or oblivion. Dolls were not a favourite, though I remember a large one, Margaret. A pram was not at all welcomed and soon abandoned. A dolls' house, however, proved very versatile. It was the centre for adventures in the person of an avatar who was the rider of a motorcycle, his conveyance being lost. I could only be represented by a figure who was clearly in no sense a doll, and the astride posture was very useful, many of my adventures taking place on horseback. My parents clearly began to understand the drift of my mind, and a subsequent well-loved present was a fort with its own garrison.

My friends in Southwell Road and its neighbourhood were not all Catholics, though some substantial Catholic families lived in the area. The largest, and something of a legend, were the Stokelds of Park Road South, with sixteen children. I did not know them, though my mother, I am not sure on what evidence, described their meal times as conducted with the discipline of a military operation. In Southwell Road, boys and girls played freely together and I enjoyed Cowboys and Indians and the acquisition of speed through a Triang scooter. I formed the idea of starting a club of my own, fortified no doubt by the reading of Enid Blyton: I identified with Julian. We were to meet in the garden shed of number 75, where I had created a den, braving large spiders and once having a white mouse as a pet. Even in those early days I believed that organisations should be built upon principle, and I drew up rules and called for a democratic election of our leader. As the garden shed belonged to me and I was the prime mover of the association, there was little doubt in my mind as to who that should be. Imagine, then, my chagrin when the Docherty family from Exeter Road, with eight members, created a majority for their eldest brother, Michael. I have no memory of what happened next and I imagine that I discreetly withdrew my labour and the venue.

More successful a venture was the great jumble sale. I had heard a great deal, at St Philomena's, about starving children in Africa, and we had a mission box at home in which we collected coins. So I organised a jumble sale for this cause, and my proud memories are supplemented by snapshots of myself, aged about eight, seated amidst the throng at the tea trolley that was my stall. We raised over £2 for the African missions, which I proudly delivered to the home of the local organiser. In the snaps of the scene there is an older girl, busily serving at another stall. Her father was arrested by mine and later imprisoned for blackmail, but it made no difference to the relationship between our families. I always felt that my father's faith was revealed in this sort of compassionate attitude. Although inevitably he was insistent that my brothers' public behaviour was beyond reproach, he never condemned others. A boy from the local remand home would come to spend Sundays at home with us. When I pressed my father about what I fondly imagined was the tough side of police life, he told me that he had once removed the handcuffs of a young offender so as not to humiliate him on a train journey, only to have him escape. The only time he had used his truncheon, he insisted, had been on night duty in the town centre, when he had thrown it at a rat. Unfortunately he missed his target, but shattered the window of a large department store.

My two brothers formed part of the walls of our family life, but they were considerably older than I and had lives of their own. From them I gained a happy sense of the different aspects of the character of the male sex but also the possibility of comradeship. Jimmy left for National Service in the RAF when I was five; the pictures he took of me in the garden at the time, pulling faces for his Kodak camera, speak clearly of his affection and protectiveness. David supported me too. When I acquired my first set of marbles and took on the local boys, I neglected to learn the rules of the game. The concept of losing those precious presents was not something I had contemplated, so the dispossession of all my marbles came as a huge shock. David, when he heard, immediately went out to play on my behalf and recovered them all, with some extras.

Strangely it never occurred to me that being a girl would deprive me of any opportunities in life. I did notice that the Docherty twins, Paul and Francis, were able to serve at the altar of St Philomena's, something clearly denied to me. Initially resentful, I examined their precise role and concluded it was not great. Certainly wearing a cassock and cotta and swinging the censor at Benediction looked at first sight attractive, but the process was repetitive. What convinced me of the essential subservience of the altar boy was when I noted that the priest, on completing his reading of the Epistle or Gospel in Latin, his back to the congregation, actually indicated by a small hand movement the timing of the response of his server: 'Deo Gratias'. This was not a demanding activity nor particularly to be envied.

Life was full of interest. I acquired a dog, Sandy, and in walks across the local common I was a secret agent, followed by mysterious representatives of foreign powers avid for my information. Foreign powers themselves, however, existed only in the newspapers, on the round black Bakelite radio, and in my mind. We did not have a car and the only international journey I heard of was a police visit, surprisingly, by my father to Sweden, on what I took to be a course led by MI5. In fact the known world was contained within a radius of perhaps twenty miles. The number 40 bus took us

15

on Thursdays, before I started school, to West Hartlepool, to visit my grandfather. The number 55 went to Durham, where I was and still am transported by the beauties of the cathedral, and on to Sunderland, where Vera's younger sister Zillah lived. Once a year we had a week's holiday, usually renting a cottage in the nearby countryside. The pre-Beeching train service to Saltburn and Whitby provided for me a mail line of interest and communication. Beyond that, knowledge came from the written or the spoken word; there was no experience of places or of people with other languages. While there was so much of vital importance in the immediate post-war world, the lack of direct contact meant that for me, in the first eleven years of my life, the acquisition of knowledge was not in any way restricted to the immediate. The volumes of *The New Book of Knowledge* opened up the far away and the past. School contributed something different.

2

At the age of four years and eight months, in September 1950, new sources of information and new skills became available, for my mother took me for the fifteen-minute walk to school: St Joseph's Roman Catholic Mixed Infants and Junior School, next to St Joseph's Church on Marton Road. I believed that this was a fresh world and that it was essentially mine; the centre of my being was with my family, but school represented an independent centre of operations. I could not see that my parents should play any part in it. My earliest humiliation in life came with my mother's determination to speak to my first teacher, Miss Carey. What was even more deeply embarrassing was the subject of the conversation: my mother was concerned that I would not fasten my liberty bodice, known to all ladies of a certain age as a strange sleeveless and buttoned garment worn next to the vest, after going to the toilet or playing games. Evidently reassured by the kind Miss Carey, I do not remember, thankfully, my mother's participation again in the adventures awaiting me at St Joseph's.

The mechanisms of learning to read and write elude my memory: I think I began at home, with the help of my parents. Certainly the two years of infants' classes seem to have gone smoothly. I know I did resent anything that I thought belittled my intellectual grasp. At the age of five,

Miss Raw asked me to find out the time for her; she gave me a wooden clock and indicated that I should go to the main school clock and move the pointers into the same positions. I was deeply insulted. I did as she asked, but on my return I held the wooden clock to my side and said 'It is ten to twelve,' to make entirely certain that she would know that I did not relish such plausible tricks.

Life, and learning, became serious in Primary 3, known as Junior 1 and Miss McIlhatton's class. This was the year of First Communion, and more frighteningly, of First Confession. I can look at myself in the class photograph, aged seven, smiling and looking comfortable with my forty-four fellow pupils. What I remember is the earnestness with which I approached the two Sacraments and the heart-searching that accompanied the journey. First of all came the Catechism, with its hundreds of questions and answers. Most of these were to be learned by heart at Primary School and formed the basis of many lessons and recitations.

Q. Who made you?
A. God made me.

Q. Why did God make you?
A. God made me to know Him, love Him and serve Him in this world, and to be happy with Him forever in the next.

This phase of Catholic learning was immensely interesting to Vera and she entered into my progress enthusiastically. From her I received a much more detailed Catechism with footnotes, which needless to say I found hugely attractive. From the pocket-sized Catechism itself I could learn many things, including the four sins crying out to Heaven for vengeance: *Wilful murder; The sin of Sodom; Oppression of the poor; and Defrauding labourers of their wages.* I could answer the question *How is Baptism given?* very easily: *Baptism is given by pouring water on the head of the child, saying at the same time these words: 'I baptise you in the name of the Father, and of the Son, and of the Holy Spirit.'* But Vera's more detailed Catechism explained that Baptism could be given by immersion and aspersion, as well as effusion. From an early stage I recognised that there is more to most seeming facts than meets the eye.

It was in preparing for Confession and Communion that I first had any personal dealings with nuns. The Church of St Philomena did have a convent of the Sisters of Charity nearby in Park Road South, and I was familiar with their striking winged headdresses. Indeed Vera helped them annually at the church bazaar. St Joseph's was led by a different order, the Sisters of Mercy, in the person of the headmistress, Sister Mary Monica, and the teacher of the top class, Sister Mary Baptist. Sister Monica and Sister Baptist checked on our seven year-olds' knowledge of the Catechism and our readiness for our First Confession, which took place in St Joseph's Church. The confessionals were at the back of the church on either side, and to hear the confessions of an entire class of forty-five pupils, two of the three resident priests were hidden behind their respective doors. The parish priest, Canon McMullen, was regarded as the tough option, though not for any obvious reason beyond seniority. Father Storey and Father McEnroe seemed quite human, despite their clerical black.

Preparing for a Confession was a serious personal business, not least because of the demand to examine one's conscience rigorously beforehand. This was something that worried Vera seriously, perhaps because by the very nature of things, Confession being very much in private, there could be no standard of comparison and no assurance that one was on the right lines. Even at seven, I took the examining of my conscience to heart. The sins crying out to Heaven for vengeance were out of my league. I also felt certain that I had not committed any mortal sins, which involved foreknowledge and obviously critical actions, such as theft or missing Mass on Sundays; they killed the soul and deserved Hell, and I could not see myself straying into that area. It was the venial sins that gave the trouble. I could not possibly regard them as trivial, not simply because, as I learned, they gave offence to God, but because they marked a failure on my part to be a true Catholic, constantly raising my mind and heart to God. Guilt entered my life: I was not concentrating hard enough, I was distracted during prayer, I had unkind thoughts about others.

The gravity of all this weighed heavily upon me and I took Confession to be a very important part of my life. After our First Confessions, we were marshalled in St Joseph's Church by Sister Monica and Sister Baptist for subsequent Confessions on something like a monthly basis, and waited in rows for our turn. The operation was slick and brooked no flexibility. One day my lot fell to Canon McMullen and, as the next person waiting in the allotted spot, I actually heard words uttered by the previous penitent. He was a boy not noted for academic interest and he confessed to talking in class. I was horrified to have overheard, unwittingly, but also because this seemed a matter totally outside the purview of the confessional. School rules could not be confused with the spiritual journey to God. My sense of my own unworthiness led me to go to Confession frequently, sometimes weekly. They were heard at St Philomena's on Saturdays, in the early evening; thence I often went alone, because Vera's concern over getting Confession right led her to go less frequently. The early evenings in the winter months were dark, and I would deliberately force myself to walk back through an unlighted alley behind the gardens of Park Road South. I was afraid of the dark, and I believed that such fear must be mastered. I was not successful in attaining this end, but the guilt and the determination that characterised my early experience of Confession are with me still.

The rigours of Confession were followed by the celebration day of First Communion, and that meant a special dress. Naturally it was to be white, but my mother was determined that it would be full-length, against my better judgement, and even had half bows of blue ribbon on the bottom of the skirt. A white veil completed the outfit. The occasion itself was complicated by the personal anguish of receiving the Host: as this was given by the priest directly into the mouth, there was the difficult question of where precisely to position the tongue. Despite the continued demands of Confession, the reception of Holy Communion marked a very significant point in the life of a Catholic child and gave a sense of membership of the full community. More important than the great day itself was the weekly Mass, when I would leave the pew with my mother to go to the altar rails and return with bowed head, sure that this was a time of special communication with God.

Time proved me right over the dimensions of the dress. At first its length seemed very attractive, as it was distinctive and special. I enjoyed wearing it for the first time after the First Communion Mass itself at Middlesbrough's Corpus Christi procession. The town was a great industrial centre, with the iron and steel works of Dorman Long and the ICI plants at Billingham and Wilton: many Irish Catholics had been attracted by work there and the Catholic presence was considerable and made visible in many schools and churches. The Corpus Christi procession was a grand affair, in which Catholic associations and schools processed behind banners. The Monstrance, containing the Host and therefore, in all our minds, the Real Presence of the Son of God, was born by a priest in a glorious cope under a canopy. Some girls in white dresses, chosen I know not how, strewed roses in front of the Monstrance. In each school contingent, the boys were dressed in their blazers and ties, and the girls in white dresses with veils. The procession wound its way through the centre of Middlesbrough and was an extraordinary demonstration of the Catholic presence in the town.

I was not much aware of prejudice or animosity between the religions of Middlesbrough. No one had indicated any displeasure or surprise when I played in Southwell Road, whether as a cowboy or for marbles, with the neighbouring children. Gradually the world of St Joseph's meant that the children I knew were mostly Catholics. There was no contact between schools; I once heard children from a Protestant school referred to as 'Proddy dogs'. But no more than that.

The glories of the full-length dress, however, quickly disappeared. The occasion was a school presentation to which parents were invited, the only time, as I recall, during my time at St Joseph's. The children of Miss McIlhatton's Primary 3 class were to perform 'A Fairy Found a Farthing'. Now I had no expectation that I would be considered for the part of the fairy, who danced throughout. We had occasional country dancing classes and I danced with George, whose feet were to be avoided. But I did look forward to joining my fellows as a daffodil, undistinguished but present on stage. My horror was great when I discovered that while everyone else could wear her white Communion dress, I was not permitted to do so because of its length. I can still remember the pain of wearing, amidst this sea of white, my pink and green best dress with the smocking on the front, a daffodil only in the green leaves and yellow cardboard flower on my head. I should have resisted the length of that dress from the first.

Miss McIlhatton's class was not just about First Confession and Communion. It was the end of Infants and the start of Junior School, and work became competitive. We were all aware that in Junior 4 (Primary 6), when we reached the august care of Sister Mary Baptist, we would sit the 11+ examination and be selected for our secondary school. The goal for the girls was Newlands Convent Grammar School. I was aware now of the processes of learning. We sat in groups determined by ability, which changed on performance. We learned many things by heart: poetry, the times tables, the Catechism. We were tested on spelling and sums regularly, passing our work to our neighbour for marking quickly. There was an emphasis on accuracy rather than imagination and I was determined that I would get everything right. There seemed no other goal. I knew I needed to know these things and there were plenty of other opportunities, outside school, to think, to read and to dream.

As the years went by and the boys in particular grew livelier, the atmosphere became tougher and canes were used. Once a boy, Jimmy, was beaten painfully, and I thought shockingly, in front of the class, because he had made a small drawing, perhaps obscene, on the cloakroom wall.

Miss Hardy of Junior 2 was caring but intimidating. Every Monday she questioned the whole class on their attendance at Sunday Mass. Although my record was faultless, the 11 o'clock at St Philomena's was clearly of lesser value than the children's Mass at 9 o'clock at St Joseph's, and her lips pursed when I made my disclosure. Nothing more was said, but inside me was an impassioned outburst that naturally I would go to Mass with my family, at a time of my parents' choice. Internally I was an independent thinker, but externally I wanted to be correct. In Mr Curtis's class, Junior 3, I sought to excel in the top group. One day it was clear that I did not know what the verb 'to consume' meant, and Mr Curtis laughed. I hated that. It was in this year, though, that I first felt very much my own person. An individual school photograph, taken when I was eight, shows me quite poised and reflective, holding a fountain pen (still capped) over the page of the exercise book in front of me and wearing a medal of St Teresa of Lisieux on my tunic.

Sometimes I was ill, with I suppose a heavy cold or what might today be called flu-like symptoms. My mother gave me all her attention, and if I felt really bad and the doctor was to be called I would be given my parents' bedroom at the front of the house, next to the little box room, which was mine. Normally the bedrooms were unheated, but now the gas fire was turned on and I had books and comics to read. Our family doctor was Doctor Pedlow, who was solid and comforting in his grey three-piece suit, with silver hair and gold-rimmed spectacles. 'What seems to be the trouble?' was his standard greeting. I was fascinated by this form of words, which conveyed his need to have practical information from the sufferer but at the same time his vastly superior knowledge. Sometimes his partner Dr Watts would come. In my mind Doctor Pedlow would never have his title abbreviated, but Dr Watts, though probably reliable, was not only Dr but he had a first name, Alan.

Unwell but rather pleased with life, fussed over and able to read, with no spelling tests, I enjoyed each of these few days in the front bedroom. I pondered the white statue of Our Lady, especially when its title was explained to me: the Immaculate Conception. Mary was the mother of Jesus, but she had not been married. I read more and discovered that Bernadette Soubirous, St Bernadette, had said she had had a vision of Our Lady, who had said to her, 'I am the Immaculate Conception.' Her reporting of these words, spoken by an ignorant peasant girl, had convinced the ecclesiastical authorities that her vision was true. I thought that, from Our Lady's point of view, it was a rather strange way to describe oneself. I could not make the intellectual bridge between the angel's visit to Mary, the Annunciation, and the birth of Jesus. There was more here than was immediately apparent, and I knew instinctively that I could not form the right questions orally. This was one for the future.

Dr Pedlow also made me think in other ways about my future. I was starting to contemplate careers at the time, and truly believed that all doors would be open. He advised me to become a dentist. He said that not enough people thought about that, and if they were interested in medicine then they immediately thought of becoming a doctor. Dentists, he said, led much more regular and peaceful lives.

Restored to health and to school, a career in medicine clearly took second place to the increasing seriousness of life in the senior class of Primary School, Junior 4. In my very first term, still only nine, we were taken to St Mary's Cathedral to file around the catafalque of Bishop Thomas Shine. As I remember, his body was embalmed, but that may be another reflection of intense imaginings. Academic work was serious too. Sister Baptist's aim was that all her girls should gain a place at the convent and her boys at the college, and that could only be achieved through success in the 11+ examination. We were tested daily. The twelve words of spelling a day were totted up, and those who achieved the full sixty correct each week were rewarded on Friday afternoon with a third-of-a-pint bottle of milk, saved from the national daily allocation to schools, and a scone. Wednesdays were spent taking the full 11+ papers, in Arithmetic, English and Intelligence, as we called it.

Our papers were returned to us and we pored over mistakes in order to eliminate them. We were placed in order in class, and I made it to first position, where I desperately wanted to remain. On the one hand, sitting in the corner in the best spot, seated next to Dennis Kelly, the cleverest boy in the class, produced an intellectual confidence, which gave me great strength. On the other hand, I believed I was unworthy of this place and would fall from it at the next test. That anxiety too remained with me and indeed, in a fundamental way, is still there.

Out of school, the search for meaning continued. When I was ten, my second brother David began his National Service. That left the back bedroom, overlooking the garden, to me. In the bottom drawer of the larger, rather forbidden dark wood wardrobe, I found the book which was to have a great influence on the next years of my life: Moriarty's *Police Law.* My first thought was to discover what the girl next door, who was a Protestant and whose parents, incredibly, owned a car, called mysteriously the facts of life. My mother had given me a pamphlet, *Dear Daughter,* which explained in comforting terms the onset of menstruation. But there was clearly much more to find out.

At home we talked all the time, but never about life's great secrets. The difficulty was that the human body never entered any conversation except in the most limited way. Even the digestive system, with its higher and lower functions, could not be mentioned. Peripheral areas, such as food and clothes, might be discussed, but food ceased to be a subject once it had reached its destination, and clothes were restricted to outer garments. Against this background, the reproductive system never stood a chance. But I believed the answers could be found. I was convinced that my father, as a detective, knew things about life that were not taught at St Joseph's. He went into parts of Middlesbrough where others did not venture and he had served on seven murder investigation teams. He must have known more.

Police Law proved full of information about life. I found the Offences against the Person Act, 1861, particularly helpful, and I pored over the definitions of buggery, sodomy and bestiality. They confirmed my belief that there was more to human relations than appeared on first encounter, but the difficulty was that they did not have a resonance with the behaviour I observed among the inhabitants of Southwell Road, Middlesbrough, still less among the occupants of Number 75. I needed more pieces for this jigsaw, but all I had was the Tuesday delivery of my mother's magazine, *Woman. Woman* was not a feisty, trend-setting paper for cutting-edge, forward-looking alpha females; it reflected the female world of 1950s Middlesbrough, and its stable-mate was entitled *Woman and Home*. It featured apple pie, to the moment of eating only, and lipstick, but only in terms of colour and application. However, it did have an agony column. Every Tuesday, I perused these letters in the hope of illumination. Sadly, they were couched in the most general terms, but they did reveal that men could be difficult and demanding. Clearly there was some link between this widely known and observed phenomenon and the Sexual Offences Act, but the intellectual gulf was still wide.

I am not sure when I realised that I would not be able to take the real 11+ that year. The local education authority stuck rigorously to the right ages, and only children in the year in which they became eleven could take the examination and move on the following year to the secondary school for which they had been selected. A few of us had not yet reached that age, and our fate was to repeat Junior 4. But what may have seemed a boring interlude proved a year of inspiring learning. We kept up with the Wednesday practice papers; by this time I was getting almost full marks in everything. But for much of the time, I was able to use the classroom library and pursue interesting topics. I wrote my autobiography, which must have been mercifully short. I found out about Sir Robert McClure and his search for the North West Passage. I wrote a study on apartheid, carefully explaining Dr Verwoerd's policies, and I referred very politely to Colonel Nasser, who after all was a living statesman, in power. I very much enjoyed this period of what seemed like intellectual independence. I remember I was given an autograph book and I had high expectations of what the headmistress would write in it. My hopes were confounded when I read 'Be good, sweet maid, and let who will be clever.' The words of Charles Kingsley did not inspire me. I never used the autograph book again.

The 11+ came. I enjoyed the actual papers, once the terror of anticipating them was over; a view of examinations which never left me. The English composition was attractive: 'A Visit to the Cinema'. I had only been to the local Gaumont once or twice, but that was enough. I set the scene by describing our welcome from the attendant, 'a blonde in slacks'. This seemed very sophisticated to an eleven-year-old in 1957. Afterwards, I remember being asked to write a letter giving my views on the nature of the examination to the Director of Education. I remember I was very damning about it, and my letter was passed round the staff room. My essential mix of intellectual determination and desperate anxiety to do well was fixed.

3

In moving to the Newlands for my secondary education I met my third order of nuns. The Faithful Companions of Jesus, founded in France in 1820, had come to Middlesbrough to assist in providing education for Catholics in 1872. Newlands Convent Grammar School was well established, just off Borough Road in the centre of the town. It was very much a convent school and very much for girls: there were no male teachers. I did not feel excluded from the company of boys, perhaps because of my two brothers, and I found no problem in moving from St Joseph's Mixed Infants and Juniors to Newlands Convent. The real differences were far more significant: the new world of specialist teaching and learning was very exciting. The headmistress, Mother Mary Monica, told my mother in my presence that she expected great things of me. I was inspired; my mother worried. *It's more important to make an apple pie than to be clever*, Vera said. I was never convinced of that.

The Newlands had a very distinctive ethos, which was created initially by the uniform, rigidly enforced. At St Joseph's there was a set dark brown tunic for the girls, with a blouse and tie, but there was much variety. Now a maroon tunic, buttoned from top to bottom, was required and accompanied by a cream blouse and striped maroon tie. There was a blazer with gold braid and badge, and, most horribly, a beret that had to be worn even when travelling to and from school. The school motto, *Fortiter et Recte, Courageously and Honourably*, was on our badge and explained to us at once. If we were in doubt about our allegiance, there was the school song:

> *Hail, alma mater, unto thee*
> *Our Newlands School, we raise*
> *Our loving hearts and proudly sing*
> *A grateful song of praise.*
>
> *Full many years have o'er thee passed*
> *In sunshine and in shade,*
> *Since loving hands first sowed the seed*
> *And deep foundations laid.*
>
> *So Fortiter et Recte*
> *Our guiding star shall be.*
> *Let honour be our motto,*
> *And courage keep us free.*

The school song was sung regularly at our daily Assemblies, which always contained a strongly worded hymn of the most Catholic kind:

> *God bless our Pope*
> *God bless our Pope*
> *God bless our Pope*
> *The Great, the Good.*

This seemed a kind of national anthem, not discriminating between the actions and characters of successive Popes. It took some time before I was able to consider the various views on the reign of Pius XII. Less ambiguous was:

> *Faith of our Fathers, holy Faith,*
> *We will be true to Thee till death,*
> *We will be true to Thee till death.*

Perhaps not mysteriously, given the Irish origin of so many Middlesbrough Catholics, we also sang:

> *Hail glorious St Patrick, dear saint of our Isle,*
> *On us thy dear children bestow a sweet smile.*
> *For though thou art high in the mansions above,*
> *On Erin's green valleys look down in thy love.*

On arrival at school each morning, in my case very proudly, on my new Palm Beach bicycle with straight handlebars, we went straight from the cloakroom to the combined Assembly Hall and gym. We sat in rows on the floor in our forms: there were three in my year of one hundred and six pupils. Until eight forty we were permitted to chat, but then the first bell rang, and for the next ten minutes we were obliged to sit in silence until we all rose with the arrival of Mother Mary Monica on the stage promptly at ten to nine. Always interested in the running of organisations, I could understand that the ten minutes of silence was useful in preventing too much exuberance and creating the right atmosphere for Assembly. I disliked this practice nonetheless, as I resented, silently, any rules that were imposed without explanation, as though on a lower form of life. Similarly I could understand that silence on the stairs was a help to good order, as was the requirement to walk always on the left, but I did hate these restraints on natural behaviour.

Externally, though, I must have seemed a model pupil. When our First Year Group was brought together at the start of the year by Mother Monica, and she asked us why our classes were called 1, 1A and Alpha, I put up my hand at once and replied that Alpha was the Greek for A, enabling her to explain that the classes were equal and not divided by ability. I took a great delight in responding immediately to questions in class, and as the questions were usually closed and factual and as I was a confirmed reader of *The New Book of Knowledge*, I almost always knew the answers. In preparing for Confession I would worry that this trait indicated that I was proud and enjoyed *showing off*, the sin of pride. In reality, though, I think I wanted to engage with my teachers and to get things right.

The considerable advance of secondary school, of course, was to be taught by specialists. Our teachers wore gowns and we stood to greet them. Each lesson began with a prayer and we stopped at noon each day to say the *Angelus*. We had exercise books with the school's name, wherein best writing was always to be used. For class notes and rough work there were jotters, and even, for special projects, hard-backed notebooks. My delight in stationery, engendered by this rich variety, has never left me, even after my computer addiction set in thirty years later. There was much learning to be done; as at St Joseph's, much of it was by heart. We learnt speeches by Shakespeare, much poetry and, of course, Latin grammar. To this day I can recite from *Kennedy's*

Latin Primer: not only the list of prepositions governing the accusative and ablative, which is only to be expected, but many of the footnotes too. None of this worried me. I believed that everything one produced in writing ought to be correct in whatever language, and that time and effort were required to get the details, like spelling, grammar and syntax, absolutely right and to be able to understand why. It did not concern me that, in French for example, I was not learning actually to communicate with a French native and that, apart from answering questions in class, I would be terrified to speak in public, and that all the authors we encountered were long dead.

Most of the teaching was solid and detailed. It involved much copying of diagrams from the blackboard, and regular testing of factual knowledge. Shakespeare and novels were usually studied by reading them round the class. However, there were inspiring and memorable times. In Form I, Mrs Hughes taught us medieval history and selected me to play William Rufus in class, in dramatic confrontation with the Pope. This I enjoyed enormously and I never forgot the importance of trying to understand the character, perspective and aims of key players in past events. Some teachers were gifted at encouraging real learning. Miss Thompson, the head of mathematics, responded to my query in a second year class about why the x-axis, in distance, clearly did not represent the speed of the train indicated on the y-axis. *You think about it and see if you can work it out*, she said. I did, and was triumphant when I realised that what the graph actually showed was the relationship between speed and braking distance.

I never in my entire school career had a meal in school. At the end of the morning's work at the Newlands, I would ride home on my trusty Palm Beach, wearing my beret of course, and after ten minutes I would be enjoying a cooked dinner in Southwell Road. I never realised at the time just how dedicated Vera was. She believed that hot meals should be prepared whatever the time of day or the demands on her, and with my father on shift work and me at school, it was often only on Sundays that we were able to sit down at the dining room table together. The dining room was in fact the living room, where I had watched the falling snow so many years before. The front room, or sitting room, which looked out onto Southwell Road, had a rather uncomfortable three-piece suite and an aged piano. It was very rarely used. For dinner in the middle of school days I would sit at the table in our kitchenette, almost a corridor, while Vera would stand at her stove in the adjacent scullery.

On Tuesdays we had choir in the middle of the day at school, conducted by the wonderful Mrs Middleton. That left only half an hour to ride home, to eat and to return. I made it, every week. Choir was very important, and led to two major musical occasions in my school life. The first was in the second year of the Newlands, when Mrs Middleton, aided by the redoubtable Miss Diamond (later Mrs Blott), staged *The Mikado*. I was a tenor, complete with bald wig and pigtail and a costume said to be on loan from D'Oyly Carte. The second was two years later, when we sang excerpts from *The Messiah* in Middlesbrough Town Hall, as an entr'acte in a performance by the Vatican organist, Fernando Germani. The power of both occasions was intense and I loved music. I had given up competing with the aged piano at an early stage, bored by the constant practising of *Silver Trumpets and Study in D Minor* for the Grade 1 piano examination. But singing was different, and eventually I even had private lessons with Mrs Middleton at her home in Saltburn on Saturday mornings.

The second and only other extra-curricular activity at the Newlands was sport, or, as we called it, 'Games'. I hated the few occasions on which we had gym, as I felt ugly and unco-ordinated. Games, however, and in particular netball, hockey and tennis were different. Although I felt the rules of netball, which stupidly did not allow running with the ball, could profitably be rewritten, I thoroughly enjoyed my role as goal defence and the playing of occasional matches against other schools. I was left back in hockey and loved the sense of giving opportunities to the wings and forwards: well I remember the description of our games mistress, Miss Carr: the team should take Old Testament advice in its attack: 'The Assyrian came down like a wolf on the fold.'

But the main business of the Newlands was naturally the lessons. We had religious instruction each day, given by our form mistress unless, as happened rarely, she was not a Catholic. Although we belonged to a convent school, we did not see many nuns. Mother Mary Monica was an Olympian figure at Assembly; Mother Winifred taught English and Sister Bridget served milk and biscuits at break. The demands of school were carried with us each evening when we took home our books, in my case in a huge haversack, together with our homework diaries. The concept of homework was new and in my case formed the rest of my life. There was no separation of the working day from the evening and the weekend. My father had painted a former kitchen cupboard base for use by me as a desk in my new back bedroom, but although I kept it well stocked with stationery, I preferred to work at the dining room table. For the first years of secondary school, this procedure was undisturbed by television. Later, when the box arrived, it meant a self-denying ordinance or the capacity to work with a lively background.

Homework came in many forms. There were exercises, in maths or languages, to be worked and corrected in class the next day. There was learning of poems or grammar, to be tested orally at the following lesson. There was the constant work of adding to the history notebook, well supported by *The New Book of Knowledge*. Weekly, there was the English composition, to be written in a special exercise book and marked out of ten in red. We were told from the first that the complex demands of such an original piece, requiring not only correctness of grammar and spelling but clear construction, arresting content and imagination, would make the highest likely mark seven out of ten. I was deeply impressed by this. Full marks for learning by heart and exercises were nothing, requiring the merest concentration. But a composition for English, and as time went on for other subjects, showed the individual mind at work in all its complexity.

Another key element of the start of secondary education was entry into a world where, it seemed to me, personal worth was determined by examination success. I was used to constant testing, particularly in relation to the 11+. But that required simply practice and technique. By contrast, subject examinations demanded considerable knowledge and recall; my view of what was capable of being learned meant that I was in a state of dread every time. I could not possibly know enough. Twice a year, at Christmas and in the summer, we sat examinations in every subject that we had studied, and were given for each a percentage and a place in class. Our overall place in class was then determined, followed by our place in the year group. On the final Assembly at the end of the autumn and summer terms, each form rose in front of the whole school. Then the places of each pupil, and her percentage average, were read out. The pupil then moved to her place physically. That first December day, in 1957, I was first in form and first in year, and I moved to the front. It was naturally deeply satisfying, but accompanied by two other feelings: the first was for those humiliated by the experience, especially for Frances who was thirty-fifth in her form and one hundred and sixth in her year. The second was the sheer terror of knowing the whole process would start again, with new knowledge, new learning, and new examinations. I thought I could never maintain my position. In fact I did, throughout my years at the Newlands, and I think I would have been devastated had I slipped a place. But at the same time I did not believe that my success would last. This moving to the front would be for the last time; the work would get too difficult for me, I was just not clever enough. So every examination I took I was convinced not only that I would not do well, but that I would fail ignominiously. This dread accompanied me throughout my examinable life and in 1973 I had to be persuaded to return to what in Oxford were called the Examination Schools after the first paper of my finals, so sure was I that I had revealed nothing but ignorance and the rest must be a waste of time.

The move from the first year was an exciting one. It had been decided to try an accelerated form of selected pupils, to be known as 3R, the R indicating Remove. I enjoyed being part of this group of just eighteen pupils and I liked the pace. At the end of the year, however, it was decided that this experiment was not successful overall, and we reverted to our original year group and I joined Form 3A. In the third year, as a result, I found much of the curriculum repetitive and I must have complained frequently and doubtless vociferously at home. My mother, after the success of the liberty bodice episode, decided, without my knowledge, to go into school to talk about this. Unsuspecting, I was invited at the end of one school day to a meeting in the staff room, at which I sat in a circle with every single one of my teachers. In turn each asked me how I was feeling about my progress in her subject and what may help. It was terrifying at the time, but in retrospect it represented an amazingly enlightened determination to meet my needs. Thereafter I was given extra work in mathematics and individual targets: I remember writing for the Latin newspaper, *Acta Diurna*, and being given an edition of Thomas á Kempis's *Imitation of Christ* for a religious project.

The quest for meaning in life and relationships started at St Joseph's continued. The study of reproduction in biology promised much but progressed no farther than the rabbit. That was in itself helpful, and supplemented by the untaught pages of the textbook on human reproduction as well as by a rereading of *Police Law*, I felt I was reasonably informed for present purposes. Hormones did not, so far as I am aware, lead into wanting to know more. There was no allowance for such at the Newlands, although the world in general seemed to see teenagers as a different set in society, with a taste for coffee bars, short and even hooped skirts, and winkle-picker shoes with high, narrow heels and desperately pointed toes.

Occasionally I stayed with my cousins in Sunderland, and little Vera, as she was known, was my age and enjoyed pop music on her transistor radio. I was more interested in visiting medieval cathedrals and abbeys. Nothing of teenage culture appeared in school, though the occasional tunic looked a little shorter than usual and a friend might one day appear with a ponytail. I was known to visit Rea's Coffee Bar in Linthorpe Road, to enjoy a Knickerbocker Glory, but this was probably related to a trip to the Dorman Museum. No girls' gossip or pop music for me. My mother did encourage me to dress in a more grown-up manner for the one special occasion in the week: Sunday Mass. I remember with a degree of shame a particular outfit of a cream coat, a matching hat with a huge brim, bordered in pink, and extremely uncomfortable shoes. My little toes have suffered ever since and my embarrassment at remembering my weekly appearance in such garments is with me still.

The austerity of my teenage self was, I think, produced by a combination of the limitations of 1950s Middlesbrough, the culture of the Newlands, and strong personal taste. I was still much interested in Catholicism and in the spiritual life, but it did not occur to me to consider entering a religious order. I prayed regularly and examined my conscience, but in all the sermons I heard and in the lives of saints I read I found no desire for any illumination other than intellectual. I remember once, in St Philomena's, looking at the light from the sun entering through the stained-glass windows. I wondered what it would be like to have a vision or at least some sign; but I dismissed the idea very quickly.

Miracles and supernatural intervention were not for me.

As the specialist subjects at school emerged more clearly my own interests changed. My early forays into *Teach Yourself Chemistry* and *Science for the Citizen* ceased when I encountered the real thing, through textbooks and with almost no laboratory experiment. Mathematics seemed a better option and remained so for some time. But then the lure of the past, through both history and Latin, grew stronger. In studying the Tudors, we were told to ignore whole chapters of our textbook because it was written by a Protestant. I was, secretly as ever, annoyed by this. Why could we not look at the differing interpretations and choose for ourselves? Latin was exciting too, and even the short passages of Cicero and Vergil to be translated for Ordinary Level held the promise of a whole world of thought and discovery. I still thought of myself as a potential scientist, though, when at the age of fifteen I was invited to speak to Mother Mary Monica. The entry to the inner sanctum and the presence filled me with awe. I was honoured to be asked if I would like to learn Greek as well as Latin and of course I agreed. No one explained the result: I would have less time for physics and chemistry and my intellectual future would certainly lie in the arts. I have never regretted this but I have always wondered.

What lay ahead in the first instance, though, were Ordinary Level examinations. I was ill for the Mocks. Perhaps the probable flu-like symptoms that seemed to be the trouble were brought on by my now long-established dread. When I was forty-seven my GP, in the new-found desire to be transparent and to communicate all, told me that dear Dr Pedlow had written in my medical records that

I was 'highly-strung'. I fear he was right. Whatever the case, I survived the examinations themselves, though I sneezed through most of them with the first onset of hay fever. When the certificate arrived, I filled in my marks, which were not printed, in very small handwriting, in pencil. I would not deface the precious official document, but they were worthy of record. By this stage, though, I was wearying of school. It was full of friends but the rules, the walking on the left, the silence on the stairs, remained. There were important moments, as when Mother Winifred encouraged me to read Tolstoy and I discovered a world much more interesting and challenging than that of Jane Austen. But generally there was not enough argument and sense of search.

I was finding that ideas excited me and actions that were not underpinned by principle, or were made using the wrong principles, made me furious. *Police Law* and the practical experience of a policeman father led me to take out books from the central library on the law, and particularly accounts of trials. I read the Craig and Bentley case of 1953, as a result of which Derek Bentley was hanged. He had been convicted of murder, as he was part of a joint enterprise of burglary, even though he did not fire the shot or have a gun. His younger associate was too young to hang. This seemed very unjust to me, and I was angry. I became a strong opponent of capital punishment, on rational grounds but also because of entering imaginatively into the final hours and moments of those hanged, always graphically described. Nothing in school compared with the interest to be found on the shelves of Middlesbrough Public Library. Perhaps the Sixth Form would be very different.

There were certainly some external differences to Sixth Form life at the Newlands. We had a new headmistress, Mother Mary of the Angels. We were allowed to wear pleated skirts, which had to touch the floor when one knelt and were of course in maroon. There were small leadership roles, such as running the stationery cupboard and presiding over the cloakrooms. The latter was no pleasure, as the rule of silence had to be imposed and, needless to say, I had no belief in it. Efforts were made, though, to make us feel that we had entered a new phase of life. I well remember Miss Diamond, or Mrs Blott as she had then become, addressing us: 'Now, girls, is the time to cultivate an educated accent.'

This statement echoed a feeling I had long had, that a local Middlesbrough accent, with its short vowel sounds, was spoken by the working class. Was I working class? I presumed I was. My father worked; my brothers worked. They were not members of professions. We lived in a small semi-detached house. We did not have a car and had only recently acquired a television. I had asked my mother this fundamental question some time ago; her view was that we were lower middle class. Did, though, education play some part in these categories? Both my parents had left school at fourteen. The few books in our home were largely mine. No one except for me was interested in classical music or went to the theatre and such topics were usually a matter for jokes. We did sit down to eat at table together, but not in the style that I had noticed in some of my friends' houses. On the other hand, other friends came from large families and lived on council estates. There were parts of Middlesbrough where I would not have ventured, where the houses were small terraces, back to back. My father said that often inside they were kept like palaces. So what did social class mean? I made my own, provisional judgement. Social class derived from low income but was manifested in style of life and above all in habit of mind and speech. Hence the need, if one wanted choices in life, to 'cultivate an educated accent'. I do not think I liked the injunction, but I seem to have followed it.

The real purpose of the Sixth Form was more advanced study and I looked forward to that. But in the end it was disappointing. I loved Latin and Greek, but my by now very few fellow pupils in the classics did not share my fascination with the languages. History was dull and the class library was lacking in interest: the public library had shown me much better things. It was interesting to read *King Lear,* of course, and to keep up with French, but the challenge was lacking and I could not see where it would lead. Two more years of this régime seemed distinctly unappealing, when I wanted to pursue something significant. University was always mentioned as the eventual goal, but that seemed to indicate more of the same. My early thoughts of becoming a nuclear physicist, and then a mathematician, had over the last three years been influenced more and more by the famous trials I had been reading and the long-standing influence of Police Law. I wondered how soon I could embark on legal training.

My father, unsurprisingly, did not have a universal respect for the profession, believing that the only good lawyers were those involved in prosecution. As ever, though, he supported me valiantly. In my reading I had identified with the barristers who spoke so eloquently in court on behalf of their clients. I had even worked out the morality of defending an accused who was guilty as charged. It did not take long to discover that a career at the Bar demanded substantial finances: I realised that social class did indeed depend not only on culture but on income. In no way deterred, I set about discovering the route to becoming a solicitor. I found out that it was possible to take articles in a firm of solicitors for five years, attending the College of Law in London during this time to take the Solicitors' Qualifying Examination, without even having Advanced Levels. There was no careers advice at school, but Middlesbrough provided a youth adviser and to him, accompanied by my father, I went.

Thus towards the end of that first autumn term in the Sixth Form, I obtained a place as an articled clerk in the firm of Doberman, Richardson and Brody, of College Chambers, Borough Road, Middlesbrough. Mother Mary of the Angels and my teachers told me that I should go to university, but I was still not impressed as no reasons were given. When the end of term came I pushed my now elderly Palm Beach through the side gate of the Newlands, and cycled home in the dreaded uniform, complete with beret, for the last time. The law awaited.

4

Mr Samuel Doberman, the senior partner of Doberman, Richardson and Broady, interviewed me one day after school. I was wearing my maroon uniform and was very nervous. He explained to me that my legal training would take five years, with two separate periods of study at the College of Law in London for the Solicitors' Qualifying Examination. I would be a trainee solicitor, technically called an articled clerk, and I would be paid £2 per week during the time I worked at College Chambers. Mr Doberman had been approached by the Youth Adviser for Middlesbrough Council and he took me on without the usual charge for articles. I have always been grateful to him for his generosity, for without this I would not have been able to embark on my legal career.

There were five other articled clerks and I was to be articled to the fifth lawyer in the firm, Mr Brian Levy. The fourth lawyer was Mr Malcolm Horsman, and for some reason I thought of these two as having first names. Mr Doberman, Mr Richardson and Mr Broady, the partners, did not. All three of them formed part of the Middlesbrough Hebrew Congregation, which had been founded in 1862 and which had acquired property in Linthorpe Road, which I passed on the way to Mass, for a new synagogue in 1938. At the time I joined the firm there were about 500 members of the congregation and Mr Doberman held an influential place in it.

Just as the Middlesbrough synagogue was a few minutes' walk from Southwell Road, so College Chambers was very close to Newlands Convent Grammar School. In both cases, there was a world of difference. Work for a prominent firm of solicitors brought me into contact with the commercial life of Middlesbrough and also the magistrates' court. I also gained a glimpse of another style of life; one of comfort and opportunity. Mr Doberman dealt in commercial property and drove a very grand car. I thought it was a Bentley but later found it was a Humber Super Snipe, the only one I remember on the streets of Middlesbrough in the early sixties. I thought him enterprising, successful and kind, and I appreciated his interest in supporting and training recruits to his profession. I regarded the firm's offices as being the very epitome of modern architecture.

It did not occur to me that in all my extensive reading of trials and newspaper law reports that I had never come across a woman with any connection with the law, apart from the occasional murderess. But I am glad to say that no one suggested to me that there was any barrier of age or sex to pursuing my choice. I had just had my seventeenth birthday when I joined my five fellow articled clerks in our base on the top floor. One of them was soon to qualify, and already wore a three-piece suit. Another had completed a law degree. They were very supportive and did not give me any impression that I was a rather unusual addition to their club. The secretarial staff, too, were very welcoming and I learned from them a huge amount on practical matters concerning the running of an office. Over the holidays, with the aid of a

Pitman's textbook, I had taught myself to touch-type on the second-hand portable typewriter I received for Christmas, and like the other articled clerks I was soon inducted into the practicalities and problems of duplicating machines. I enjoyed the quest for accuracy and method and I saw the virtues of a good filing system.

It was a fascinating life for a seventeen-year-old. I travelled around the solicitors' offices in Middlesbrough, completing property purchases for Mr Broady. He did not drive a Bentley: he was the youngest partner and he was a modest, hard-working and efficient conveyancer. Often I held a watching brief in the local magistrates' court where we had a client with a third-party interest: the prosecuting solicitor knew my father and would pass me the complete file for my note. I found this most instructive. I liaised with a local furniture company over the management of their bad debts and for the first time realised the financial challenges faced by many of the town's families.

Best of all, though, was the litigation. Mr Richardson was the partner in charge of that. Lively, clever and contentious, he drove a Rover, and he wanted to win. I was thrilled that he was handling a matter that would appear in the Law Reports, for it dealt with an extension to building contractors of the duty of care established in the famous snail-in-the-ginger-beer-bottle case, Donoghue vs Stevenson. He drove me to York Assizes, where the High Court was in session, and he talked me through the case on the way. I shall never forget listening to Mr Justice Nield delivering his reserved judgement in favour of our client, and imagining how it would appear in the Law Reports. Perhaps one day Mr Justice Nield, whom I had just seen in his elegant wig, would become a Lord Justice of Appeal. He might even be mentioned in future legal textbooks that described this case in the immortal words: 'Nield J., as he then was'. I regarded this as the most complimentary way of referring to a human being that I could ever imagine. In fact Sir Basil Nield remained a judge of the High Court of Justice and his obituary in the *Daily Telegraph* described him as 'lawyer, churchman, politician, soldier and bon viveur'. There was much more to the man than my idealised portrait of the brilliant intellectual judge.

The academic year 1963–64 was the one in which I was to study for Part I of the Law Society's Qualifying Examination for Solicitors, at the College of Law in Lancaster Gate, London. I received a state grant for tuition and maintenance to fund this, as university students did. It was the year in which I would have been in Upper 6, studying for my Advanced Levels. At the College of Law I would be studying with a wide range of students; some young articled clerks like myself, some much older legal executives who had decided to qualify as solicitors, and some with university degrees in subjects other than law who had decided to enter the profession. Part I of the Qualifying Examination represented academic law and included subjects such as the English legal system, contract, tort, criminal law and real property; Part II was generally taken towards the end of the period of articles, and represented the practical skills required of a solicitor.

Intellectually I was avid to get to grips with the law; personally and socially I was not ready for what was essentially undergraduate life in London. Where was I to stay? Unexpectedly my former headmistress Mother Mary Monica rang my home. She had heard of my plans and had two suggestions: there were inter-collegiate halls of residence for students at the University of London specifically for Catholics: one was run by Opus Dei, the other by the Canonesses of St Augustine. I had only the vaguest idea of the constitution and aims of Opus Dei, but I had the idea that its lay members did not reveal their affiliation. I did not like this. Of the canonesses I had no information whatsoever, but their hostel was in Cromwell Road, South Kensington. It very well situated for the College of Law, it came recommended and it seemed a safe haven. So at the age of seventeen I came to London and into contact with my fourth order of nuns.

At first I regarded More House as simply a very good and comfortable place to sleep and work. Of London I saw practically nothing, beyond the daily walk to Lancaster Gate. Once an articled clerk from College Chambers was visiting and he took me around the City. I could not break the tie with my parents and I went home for the weekend every Friday afternoon: my mother had cashed in an insurance policy she had taken out on my behalf to make the journeys possible. I had a room of my own at More House, not dissimilar from my bedroom at home except that it had a single armchair and a washbasin. I was able to go to Mass in the chapel, wearing a black lace mantilla instead of an embarrassing hat. The College of Law offered one lecture of one and a half hours each day, which was compulsory. We were recommended, in addition, to read for six hours. Although there were libraries in which I could have worked, I had no introduction to this next stage of academic life and I sought to mirror in my room at More House the conditions in which I had worked at 75 Southwell Road. Of course I would work there for six hours a day – at least. I acquired the files and the notebooks, and I built up a decent library of legal textbooks of my own together with my particular joy, volumes of relevant cases from the Law Reports.

The judge who filled me with the greatest delight first lit up my mind in my year at the College of Law, but I never saw him in the flesh. It was Lord Denning, whose judgements I admired for their wit, their learning and their challenge. I was filled with enthusiasm when I read his judgement in the High Trees House case, which made the law of contract sing. Although I would never have used the words, he seemed to me what a young person today would certainly describe as 'cool', even perhaps 'funky'. His language was urbane and his perspective always his own. This private legal reading supplemented the solid lectures we were given at Lancaster Gate. There were no questions and plenty of information, which I noted with care. Regularly one lecture period was devoted to an essay, written under examination conditions. Schooled at St Joseph's and the Newlands, I expected no different, though the dread remained. I did well and my essays were noticed.

Still eighteen, I had completed nearly two years of articles and I had passed Part I of the Solicitors' Qualifying Examination. I received distinctions in criminal law, doubtless thanks to my early reading of Moriarty's *Police Law*, and in contract, perhaps as a result of my fascination with the cases of Lord Denning. Who was to be my role model for the future? Mr Doberman, rich, successful and kind? Mr Richardson, clever and litigious? Mr Broady, modest and competent? Well, none of them, as it happened. Mr Justice Nield represented the summit of my legal ambitions.

I admit there were moments when I thought that perhaps I too might one day be described as 'McClure J., as she then was', but Lord Denning was out of reach. He was a brilliant, other-worldly figure one only read about in books. Indeed I did not even know how to become Mr Justice Nield: the career path in that direction was not clear to an eighteen-year-old girl articled clerk in Middlesbrough in 1964.

But I knew these were flights of fancy. The religious world of Middlesbrough had continued strongly at More House and I had come into contact with another religious order dedicated to education, the Canonesses of St Augustine. The spiritual search that had been part of my life since First Confession was now extended by the intellectual enquiry encouraged by Mother Mary Edith, who ran weekly seminars in More House for the students. I felt appallingly ignorant and provincial, an uncultured girl from a northern industrial town. It seemed a time of great excitement and change. John Kennedy, the first Catholic president of the USA, was assassinated in November 1963, during my first term. The Second Vatican Council had been opened by Pope John xxiii in 1962 and reform of the Church was widely discussed, especially concerning the role of women. There was a sense of discovery in other fields: I remember one articulate participant at the More House seminars declaring that she was sure that the most important scientific advances ahead lay in the field of genetics. I wanted to be part of all this: of the debate, of the reform, of the spirit of enquiry.

I realised I must go to university. I had no more than the building blocks of understanding: I needed to learn and discuss and argue. I was also looking for an absolute commitment of my life, one which would satisfy the urge I had felt since those early days in Miss McIlhatton's class: I had been made to know God and no purpose in life could be higher than this. The backdrop to my extensive notes and reading of legal cases was the sense that perhaps I had a vocation to become a nun. I knew that such a calling was precisely that: something that came from God and was stronger than me. Equally I believed that I had been given a mind to consider this for myself and to respond properly.

The Canonesses of St Augustine seemed clearly and without much debate the order I would join. The intellectual world I had joined in London was to me of a different character from that of Middlesbrough, which now looked narrow and confined. I discovered more about the order: it had been established by Pierre Fourier, who had reformed the Canons of St Augustine in late sixteenth-century France, and had worked with Alix le Clerc to found the Canonesses. Unusually the nuns took a fourth vow: that of education was added to poverty, chastity and obedience. Mother Mary Edith explained that were I to enter as a postulant, once my novitiate was complete I would be sent to university and as a professed nun I would teach. The order ran a hall of residence for students at the University of Cambridge as well as in London.

It was a huge dilemma. I loved my legal studies, but I knew now I should have taken a law degree. I was on the path to becoming a solicitor, a profession I much respected but one that seemed to me to be concerned with the smooth running and good order of society and business. I wanted to contemplate the infinite and to find the perfect life. I pondered the issues at More House, on the train from King's Cross to Darlington each Friday, at home in Middlesbrough at the weekend. I asked advice from those I trusted and in Confession. Secretly I hoped that my parents would suggest that I went to university first, to gain more experience of life. I was only eighteen: was this too soon to commit myself to the life of a nun?

Vera and Jim did not dissuade me. For Vera certainly, and probably for Jim too, this really was a question of vocation. If God was calling me to be a nun, then their role was to support and in no sense to dissuade me. It must have been a terrible time for them, as the novitiate house was in Kent, very far from Middlesbrough by public transport. The order, although committed to education, was contemplative. I would enter the enclosure and they would see me rarely. I thought and I prayed. Then I decided: I would try my vocation with the canonesses. I wanted to respond to God's call and to become a nun.

5

In becoming a postulant with the Canonesses of St Augustine of the Congregation of Our Lady in their novitiate house, called 'Les Oiseaux', at Westgate-on-Sea, close to Margate in Kent, I was again moving to a town that I never really knew. The preparations for what I intended to be a lifetime were swift, as there was only a short space between the end of my final term at the College of Law, with the last set of examinations, and my entry with two other postulants into the convent at Westgate at the beginning of September 1964. I was given a list of required items, including sheets, towels and black laced shoes. I can only begin to envisage what this process must have been like for my parents, and in particular my mother's dark imaginings.

I do not remember the journey from Middlesbrough through London down to Kent and the Isle of Thanet, nor my first view of Westgate and the conventual buildings on Canterbury Road. The canonesses had been expelled from France as a result of the anti-clerical laws of 1904, and they had set up their convent and school in Westgate on the model of their house in Paris. The Couvent des Oiseaux in the rue de Sèvres had been a prison during the Terror with, improbably, a garden full of exotic birds. The canonesses had acquired it in 1824 and set up a school there for girls *de bonne famille* – sometimes of very good family indeed.

Occasionally even in their English exile and for all their high ideals there was a sense of the French aristocracy about the canonesses. In the Sacristy was a chalice donated to them by Napoleon III.

The land they owned on Canterbury Road lay on the outskirts of Westgate, itself a small seaside town of a few thousand inhabitants on the borders of its much more prominent resort neighbour, Margate. The architect of the buildings of Les Oiseaux was F.A. Walters, noted for more than fifty Roman Catholic churches, who between 1905 and 1915 erected the convent, chapel, school and presbytery. The Conservation Appraisal Report of 2006 paints an attractive picture of the site: 'situated within mature gardens and a large area of open land bordered by mature trees, sycamore, beech and horse chestnut. A fine high brick wall with stone coping surrounds most of the property . . .' That fine wall would mark the dimensions of my physical world, though very little time was spent in the mature gardens.

I parted with my parents outside the enclosure: I would now be given the name of Sister St Ann. They promised to see me whenever a visit was allowed, and they did. Every month they had one and a half hours with me in the parlour. For this they journeyed overnight by bus from Middlesbrough, then crossed London and took the train during the morning to Westgate. At the end of their ninety minutes they took the train back, and returned to Middlesbrough by the overnight bus the same day. It must have been uncomfortable and exhausting but it meant everything to them and to me. Each time they must have thought, as they left, that they would never see me at home again.

The door to the enclosure, where no one who was not a member of the community could set foot, was at the right of the chapel and part of the indoor cloister. The door gave unromantically onto a stone staircase and each floor marked a new area: first, the infirmary, ruled by Mother Sebastian, second, the community floor, for professed nuns, and at the top the novitiate and scholasticate. The novitiate included postulants, novices in their first canonical year and novices in their second apostolic year, when normally they would be sent to another house of the canonesses but would return out of term-time. The scholastics were nuns who had taken their first vows and would do so annually until their final profession: for three years they lived in the scholasticate under the same mistress of novices, distinguished from the novices by black rather then white veils.

The long top floor housed the individual cells. They were identical in size and had sparse furnishings. The bed, with a crucifix at its head, was narrow with white coverings on a metal frame. There was one upright chair and a l arge and dominating piece of furniture known as a *meuble*, another Parisian echo. The *meuble* was a large and heavy bureau, with a lift-down lid revealing an enamelled metal basin with a jug for fetching water, and below capacious drawers. In my head I fought my disappointment at the absence of a desk. For me a bedroom was a place for private work: I had not realised what communal life really meant. I changed into the postulant's garb: a calf-length, full black skirt, a white blouse with a black cardigan, black shoes and stockings and a simple veil to tie at the back of the head, covering most of the hair but leaving a little showing over the forehead. I did not feel like a nun but I knew the journey had begun.

I was shown the rest of the novitiate by my *bonne ange,* Mother Mary Elizabeth. She explained that we were all sisters; 'Mother' was a title for the school and for outsiders, but in the novitiate she was Sister Elizabeth and, more familiarly, *soeur.* We walked from the line of facing, closed cells, passing the scholasticate, which I was very relieved to see clearly provided a desk for each nun. Then came the large room for the novices and postulants, in which everyone gathered for prayer at the end of the day. It was large, light and airy, and it had bookshelves filled with books at one end. This was a delight and a reassurance. At one end was the altar, with a very large statue of Our Lady flanked by candlesticks and fresh flowers. The other side of the room held desks for the novices and postulants and I was shown mine. My world had contracted in size and in personal ownership, but already in this short tour I could see my physical space and how, in a world in which I had abandoned everything, I could have a place of my own and the tools to read and write.

The tour continued. Outside the novitiate was the common, where the necessities of life (I immediately spotted the pens and paper) were stored. Devout nuns asked permission to take a new item, confirming their intention to be entirely without personal possessions. To this end, the mistress of novices had a session each afternoon for permissions, where, kneeling on the floor, her agreement to these acquisitions could be sought. Indeed her room was just around the corner. Mother Mary Teresa, a Frenchwoman, was mistress of novices and indeed scholastics, though her title was usually restricted to the former. To her fellow professed she was Sister Teresa; to us she was 'Mother', to be referred to in the third person as 'Our Mother Mistress'. She signed any card or written communication in this style: OMM. All letters home and anywhere else, which would be infrequent, were to be left unsealed, so that she could read them; similarly she could read all in-coming mail. Next to her room was a scullery where cleaning materials were kept and where water was obtained at night for washing in the enamelled bowl in each meuble. Adjacent were the toilets, known familiarly as 'the Little Ways'. Apparently, in some part of the house, a picture of Saint Teresa of Lisieux had hung close to the toilets. She had recommended famously the life of hidden virtue, 'the Little Way'. Hence the familiar name generally applied to these conveniences.

Silence obtained in the novitiate, as indeed it did everywhere in the convent except for the twice-daily periods of recreation, for teaching in the school, and for essential communications. At night the Great Silence descended, when no word was spoken and the only essential communication, presumably, would have been 'Fire!' All of this was explained to me in the kindest of terms by my good angel, while I was greeted, in what was clearly essential communication, most warmly by the novices and scholastics. It was a very different world.

The day began stridently with an electric bell ringing throughout the enclosure at 6 am. The expected response was to arise immediately with a prayer, and to fetch water for washing from the scullery along the corridor. A dressing gown could be worn, and novices and professed covered their shaven heads with a white scarf. The warning bell for the start of meditation was rung in chapel at 6.25 am with what were called small *coups;* the big *coups,* with full strikes of the bell, followed at 6.30 am. A member of the novitiate was bell ringer each week and it was a little time before I was inducted into this process, first of all as an apprentice. The appointment demanded skill in pulling the heavy rope sensitively and immaculate time keeping.

Meditation each morning was set for half an hour. On Sundays we rose at 6.30 am and chose our own time in the morning, but on the other six days of the week it was set. The community spread itself throughout the splendid chapel, early twentieth- century in date but Early Decorated Gothic in style. Some read, seated on their bench, others knelt. A number were very still and upright in their kneeling position and that is the posture I sought to emulate. From the first, I thought the periods of meditation lay at the heart of my vocation. This was contemplation, the opening of the mind to God. I saw it in no other way. Spiritual reading was for other times and places, to help in the life-long process of putting oneself in contact with the omniscient, ineffable, yet personal Being. During this time I did not think about Jesus of Nazareth, or the Gospels, or Catholic teaching. I tried to commune with God. It was, needless to say, a battle against bodily discomfort, a desire to return to sleep, and the lure of other thoughts. But contemplation, I believed, was the essence of religious life.

The *coups,* small and big, rang out again at 6.55 and 7.00 am, and the first part of the Divine Office, the liturgy of readings and psalms in use since the late 5th century to bless the hours of the day, began. As a teaching order, Matins was not held in the night but *anticipated* and had taken place the previous evening. For chanting the Office, the community separated itself into the facing choir stalls, presided over by Reverend Mother from her impressive place at the back, facing the altar. The stalls were elegant and well carved. Each nun had her own position, designated from the first, and where members were absent because of school duties or illness, then the gaps were swiftly filled in order. Position was determined by year of entry to the order. When, as was at that time usual, there were several entries in the same year, the oldest took priority. Thus I was the youngest postulant of three and would maintain in this most junior position for the entire year, until the next intake. Place in the community determined every movement, even to opening and going through doors. I was last every time.

Office began when the choir mistress, who was also Our Mother Mistress, blew gently on her tuning device and we all rose to face each other. Each week a member of the professed who had taken final vows led the office. After meditation, this was the next most significant series of acts of the day for me, for I loved the Office: its language, its richness, its entry into the mysteries of the Christian year. I found the Latin especially beautiful, the result of my enjoyment of the subject at school and from the Latin Mass heard so often in St Philomena's. At this time of day we chanted three of the Hours, Lauds, Prime and Terce, and Mass began at 7.30 am with the arrival of our priest and an elderly server.

From the first, the absolute necessity of a male priest to celebrate Mass, and even a male server, began to seem very strange to me. At St Philomena's, going to Mass meant entering a world which belonged naturally to priests, who formed their own household in the presbytery and were dedicated to their calling. But the convent was for the community who had chosen to live there, and we had a history and commitment of our own. We had just meditated and said the Divine Office. Why, then, did we need a priest who was always a man to celebrate the Eucharist? In the very month I entered Westgate, the Second Vatican Council had voted by a large majority that supreme authority in the Church lay not simply with the Pope but with bishops as a whole, including him. It seemed a very exciting time of reform and now that I had changed my life to enter a religious community, I felt a living member of that process. I believed that the place of women in the Church must inevitably be recognised. Strangely, then, the Mass which had been at the heart of my religious experience at St Philomena's and at More House, was less the focus of my intense spiritual longing when I became a nun, though it remained in my mind as the central act of the Christian community.

At 8 o'clock, two hours after it had risen, the community went to breakfast in the refectory. This was a fine panelled room, with a high table for Reverend Mother at the top, flanked by the pulpit for the reader. Long tables ran down either side, leaving the middle for serving trolleys. We sat in our assigned places, with sections for the novitiate presided over by Mother Teresa, for the professed community, and for the lay sisters. These last, who were not given the title of Mother, were professed members of the community: they did not teach or take part in the Office, but carried out the major domestic work of the convent. Many were from Ireland, as I remember, and were not highly educated. I was told, I do not know with what truth, that they were placed together at table because their eating habits made others uncomfortable. They were extremely hard working and seemed happy and satisfied with their lot, but I could not understand this fundamental division. It was hard to see why, in an order devoted to education, that a section of its members should not be given further education and should be simply required to repeat Our Fathers and Hail Maries while the choir nuns enjoyed the beauties and the depth of the Divine Office.

Meals were taken in silence, except on the great feast days. At lunch, after Grace had been said, there was a reader, who read at the will and under the correction of Reverend Mother. This could be a chapter of a book with Catholic or spiritual content but sometimes it was a chosen piece from a newspaper. Most of the community were teachers and needed to be kept informed about the world. Soon I entered the list of readers myself and much enjoyed the process. The reader ate privately after the meal, which was presented to the community in large dishes, from which a serving would be taken into each person's single pottery plate. This was shaped rather like a dog bowl and thus could accommodate any foodstuff: soup, meat or sweet. Bread was served and it was possible to use it to clean the plate, at least to some degree, between courses.

I was very surprised by the large quantity of food. Fasting I had taken to be a key element in a truly religious life, where bodily urges were rigidly controlled. On the contrary: each person was required to take a standard portion of every item, regardless of taste. The mistress of novices, the senior member of the scholasticate, or the *bonnes anges* of the postulants, ensured that this practice was followed. Perhaps the true penance lay in eating regardless of the quality of the food. The lay sister in charge of the kitchen and her helpers were zealous but not trained. One dish I remember in particular was colloquially known as 'Nuns' Graveyard'. It consisted of a large serving dish filled with the mess of spinach left over from a previous meal, in which hard-boiled eggs, themselves remaindered, stood like grave stones. One such meal did indeed produce widespread sickness but fortunately did not live up to its name.

The refectory was also the scene of public penance, something of an embarrassment when first observed. There were three broad types. In the first, the penitent would kneel in front of the community, in the centre of the floor before Reverend Mother, and would hold her arms outstretched during Grace. In some circumstances she might also then publicly confess a fault. In the second, the nun would wear a bandage, known as the *bandeau*, over her eyes throughout the meal, in a position that allowed her to peer down at her plate but see little more. It was very disconcerting, I found, to be seated opposite such a penitent. Finally, a nun might position herself kneeling at the end of the meal at the entrance to the refectory. She would then kiss the black-leather-clad feet of each professed nun as she left. These penances were generally undertaken by the wish of the nun herself, and with the permission of the Reverend Mother or mistress of novices, as the case might be. The whip which I was to leave in that Oxford dustbin in 1970 was to be used in private, with clear instructions: kneeling on the floor of one's cell, while saying the Lord's Prayer, hitting the one's bare back 'as if one were a donkey'.

The main work of the day took place in the mornings, after breakfast, and after lunch. For most of the nuns, from the postulants upwards, that meant teaching in the school.

As the majority of pupils were boarders, those involved in their care at particular times were simply excused the relevant service or meeting, with the Office or meditation to be made up at a different time. I was to find out my own role in the school for my first year as a postulant very quickly. After the morning's work, Sext and None were said at 12.10 pm and were followed by lunch. Then there was the first of two periods of recreation, about half an hour in length, when conversation was allowed. Talk was, however, general, and led by Mother Teresa; particular friendships and hence private chat were always discouraged. The lunchtime period of recreation was taken on foot, either in the grounds or, if too cold or wet, in the indoor cloister. For a postulant this resulted in difficult manoeuvres. Our Mother Mistress and the senior scholastics always walked forwards, in a group; the rest of us novices and postulants walked backwards. It was not easy and not at all recreational.

The afternoon brought more work and lessons, and tea was a quick bite of bread and jam, taken standing in the refectory. Eating elsewhere was forbidden. The mistress of novices then fitted in her time for permissions, and for a separate session with the novices and postulants and with the scholastics known as 'novitiate' and 'scholasticate', after which she would expound some religious theme. Vespers came at 4.15 pm, and at 6.25 pm the bell for meditation rang again, to be followed by the Matins of the following day. After supper in the refectory there was the second period of recreation, lasting perhaps three quarters of an hour. This was enjoyed seated in a circle, again with the conversation being led by Mother Teresa. Each of us had a workbasket and was expected to get on with sewing, either special embroidery or our own mending. I had experienced needlework at the Newlands for my first two years of secondary education and my report had read 'Theory excellent. Practical work needs more practice.' I had not seen fit to heed this advice and this aspect of recreation did not appeal.

Towards the end of the period, those of us who were sleeping in the dormitories with the pupils took their leave. They knelt before Mother Teresa, who made the Sign of the Cross on their foreheads. The atmosphere was gentle and friendly. At 8.45 pm the bell for Compline, the last Office of the day, was rung and we all filed into chapel. At its end, the Great Silence descended and, after a short prayer together kneeling in front of Our Lady in the Novitiate, we all repaired to our cells to prepare for bed. It had been a long and very structured day, and so would every other be.

6

For all of us there comes a time, probably early in adult life, when we question the faith which we have inherited. Although we speak of our faith as though it were coherent and ordered, it is more likely to be a huge amorphous thing, composed of the words of our parents, teachers and clergy; of books we have read; services we have attended; thoughts we have had; moments of inspiration that have come to us in all manner of ways. Perhaps until this point of questioning we have thought of our inheritance of faith as the inheritance of faith, something accessible in the same way to all our generation; but the time must come when we perceive the fragmentary nature of our own experience; its weakness and its limitations, compared with the rich inheritance that is shared. There comes to all of us the defining moment when we realise the complexity and difficulty of faith as something that is not ours alone, but which has to be made our own if it is to have meaning in our lives. Indeed it may be that for some of us the acceptance that faith will never be a simple thing, that it is not a solid, immovable foundation upon which we can stand firm despite the problems and the griefs of life, but is in itself a terrible journey, a search for understanding which becomes more and more difficult as we peel the layers of what we have heard and read and of what we do and do not believe.

For me one such moment in the search for faith and understanding came in that first year as a postulant, now aged nineteen, when I thought I had chosen a path that was the final fulfilment of the faith that I had inherited. It took place in the lofty chapel at Westgate on the occasion of Tenebrae, one of the great offices of Holy Week. At Tenebrae the hours of Matins and Lauds were combined, and the psalms and readings were sung. The chapel was sombre and undecorated; the community, of course, in black habits. At the end of the dark wooden stalls was a large branched candlestick, and at the end of each psalm one candle was extinguished. As the youngest postulant, Sister St Ann, I was to sing in Latin the first lesson, which was taken from the Book of Lamentations. The writer, probably a contemporary of the prophet Jeremiah, evoked the horror and the sadness of the destruction of Jerusalem by the forces of Nebuchadnezzar in 587 BC.

Quomodo sedet sola civitas plena populo: facta est quasi vidua domina gentium: princeps provinciarum facta est sub tributo.

How is it that the city once full of people now stands alone? The queen of the nations has become like a widow; the chief of the provinces now lies under a yoke.

I thought it was incredibly beautiful and the words of sadness so appropriate to an evocation of the lonely death of Jesus on the cross:

Non est qui consoletur eam ex omnibus caris eius: omnes amici eius spreverunt eam.

There is no one to comfort her from all those who have loved her; all her friends have spurned her.

These words brought together the fragments of intense experience of my childhood and youth, the extracts from poems and the passages from oratorios:

O vos omnes, qui transitis per viam, attendite, et videte si est dolor sicut dolor meus.

All of you, who pass by on this road, look and see, if there be any sorrow like unto my sorrow.

It was in reflecting on the inspiration of this moment that I first came to see the complexity of the inheritance of faith. A religious community of women in Kent in 1965 was listening to a poem written in Hebrew in the early 6th century bc, translated into the dead language of Latin unknown to the poet, and referring it easily to the death of a young Jew in Palestine that took place around 30 AD. Within this brief and beautiful passage were the extraordinary problems of a text that had survived for 2,500 years in a variety of forms, and had somehow passed from generation to generation, from language to language, and had been a source of questioning, of inspiration, of meaning to countless individuals from a series of immensely different cultural backgrounds. Faith can mean many things, but from then on it became for me a search for meaning in the

Scriptures, a search that throughout all the centuries had to be undertaken in each generation.

I had the opportunity each day to pursue these thoughts at Mass and at the hours of the Divine Office. But meditation, an hour a day and three hours during special times of retreat, was intended to be devoted to intense mental prayer, quite distinct in my mind from spiritual reading. It was the central process by which each of us was to aim at a dialogue with God, and one of the principal means by which we were to hold our own selves in contempt and to strive to ignore the material world. At 6.30 am, in the darkened chapel, black figures would be kneeling, upright and still. As a postulant I marvelled at the impenetrability of their thoughts: soon I began to realise just how tangled and difficult the human mind can be when it is forced in unremitting discomfort to ponder the absolute. We were encouraged to note our thoughts and problems on these occasions, so that we could discuss them in a weekly individual meeting with Our Mother Mistress, our sole spiritual director. It was during these regular hours of meditation that I tried to force my mind to accept that I must despise myself, my thoughts, my aims, my ideas: we were expected to become, as our late sixteenth-century constitutions told us, 'like soft wax, which yielding to the hand that moulds it, receives whatever shape is desired'. This shape was to be decided by our novice mistress: each of us had simply to obey her without thought and to accept what she wished us to do or be or become.

Let them take example from a lifeless body which, even though mocked or insulted, offers no resistance; or from a little picture which can be shifted at will; or let them be like clay in the potter's hand, like a staff in the hands of an old woman who uses it according to her needs and puts it where it can best help her; like a tool belonging to a workman, who takes it up, throws it aside or puts it where he pleases in the workshop, the tool neither objecting or murmuring. The sight or mention of any of these objects should be to them a reminder of that indifference and obedience which it must be their constant care to practise devoutly.

I saw the conflict between unquestioning obedience and the lure of taking one's own moral decisions early on. An aged and unwell professed nun was in charge of the French library, containing large, antique volumes brought from the French house in 1904. The French library opened into the cloister, and I saw her labouring as she climbed ladders and tried to move heavy books. Without thinking I offered to help, and did so daily whenever I had the chance. Once this was discovered I was soundly rebuked for daring to take action without the permission demanded by obedience. I did have my own practical work: firstly sweeping the four flights of stone stairs from the cloister on the ground floor to the novitiate at the top. This was hard and dusty work, especially in the hay fever season when I was already sneezing! Secondly I took charge of the candles on the altar. That meant ensuring the stumps inserted into mock candles endured for the requisite time at Mass. I well remember one unfortunate occasion when I had underestimated for High Mass (six tall candlesticks on the High Altar) and watched dismally as they went out one by one.

But there was also the fourth vow of the Canonesses of St Augustine: that of education. Anyone who has persevered so far, or who alights on this page by chance, must undertake not to reveal the following account of my life as a teacher to the General Teaching Council for Scotland, of which I am proud to be a member. Nor to Her Majesty's Inspectors of Education in Scotland, in case those who have observed my conduct as a head teacher for many years feel able to say, 'Aha! I thought as much. Not trained at all.'

I have a response to any well justified criticism: it lies in a copy of the Full Inspection Report of Les Oiseaux Convent School No. 6031, following a visit by a team of six of HM Inspectors to the school on 27–29 October 1964. There I am on the staff list:

Part-time:

Sister St Ann   Some History (Junior Forms);
                          Latin to Form 1

I was eighteen. I had no Advanced Levels and it could be said that my Part I Solicitors' Qualifying Examinations were not directly relevant. However, I was relieved to hear at the staff meeting convened by the headmistress, Mother St Paul, that the inspectors took the view that I had 'the makings of a good teacher'. So there!

I remember their visit well. Two of them sat in on a primary lesson where we were drawing Norman castles. Others came to a short play on the workings of relations between lords and tenants and saw me coping with the questions afterwards, especially from very bright Hilary in Junior 3, who wanted to know how exactly feudal dues were calculated, with an example. Anne-Marie starred, as I expected, in Form 1 Latin. *Bene!* I had many questions for the inspectors who observed my classes on suitable approaches, and they were patient and extremely helpful.

I loved teaching: the research, the finding of creative ways of communication, and the lively interest of pupils. This joy continued through my six years as a nun, even when I was asked to teach Upper 4B mathematics. Well, I did have an Ordinary Level. I remember that I felt the pupils believed that maths was boring and unnecessary, so I asked my Dad to send me his gas bill so I could explain its relevance for all. The extra-curricular life of the school was rewarding too: I started a drama club at once. There was also the pastoral care. The regime was strict and every morning dormitories were inspected to ensure that beds had hospital corners and toiletries were properly ordered and suitable. I looked after Sacred Heart Dormitory, with thirty-five cubicles each surrounded by a white curtain. A nun always slept close to the girls in case of emergency. I tried Sacred Heart but was awake all night. I was entrusted with putting Holy Angels, the youngest pupils, to bed, and I was given a tiny room in the Crow's Nest where older girls enjoyed study bedrooms for which HM Inspectors 'found much to praise'.

I entered the novitiate with determination, when the image of becoming a Bride of Christ took the form of the postulant entering the chapel dressed as a bride in white, on the arm of her father. It must have been an incredible experience for my parents when my father walked away and my withdrawal from the world was symbolised by the cutting of a lock of my hair, and an exit from the chapel clad entirely in black, with even my face covered. My return, in the habit and with the white veil of a novice, was met with joy; their sense of loss must have been profound. Family matters were no longer for me, even when my sister-in-law committed suicide and left her three children to be brought up by my brother. At least my parents did not have to endure a ceremony for final vows, when the new professed first lay under a pall to signify her death to the world.

As a novice the teaching of music entered my life, through the Ward Method of Music, invented in the USA and developed in England at the Cambridge Centre run by Mother Thomas More at the canonesses' Lady Margaret House. Under her direction I took classes in the school years 1965–1966, 1967–1968 and 1968–1969 and I still have the detailed records of class visits: 'Excellent work . . . good teacher-pupil relationships . . . Charlotte and Vanessa had ever so many questions!'

The success of the work of Mother Thomas More gave me an unexpected experience in my novitiate year, 1966–1967, when she ran a conference in Dublin and asked for me to demonstrate. So I was allowed to wear a black veil, to the great shock of the nuns of the Irish house where we stayed. I had to fly to Ireland alone, the first time I had ever flown. Arriving in Dublin airport at midnight, I did not know where to go; the lights were going out. I discovered the reverence given even to unworthy nuns like me in Ireland: the general manager handed me the key to the First Class lounge and told me to lock myself in and make myself comfortable until the morning. Next morning, when I discovered my destination, a taxi driver gave me an extended tour of Dublin, refusing to take any fare at all. I enjoyed the conference, which went well; behind the scenes, though, a lawyer arrived from the USA to complain of copyright infringement in the use of the original Ward Method materials. My understanding of the complexities of life increased.

The Apostolic Year, before first vows, was another kind of experience. Sister Clare, for instance, was sent to the canonesses' house in Uganda for hers. I went to Lady Margaret House in Cambridge. Mother Thomas More was based there and Mother St Paul had become its Mother Superior. It was recognised that one day I would be sent to university, ideally to Cambridge, so I was allowed to work at Advanced Level history. Once a week, in the evening, I cycled to the Cambridgeshire College of Arts and Technology in full habit, for the adult education course. Needless to say I took this extremely seriously, read many books and wrote long essays: it paid off.

My role in the Cambridge community was rather different. The Divine Office was superb despite the small size of the community: Mother Thomas More, better known as Dr Mary Berry, was hugely influential in reviving Gregorian chant in Britain and abroad, and was soon to become a fellow and head of the music faculty at Newnham College. Students at Lady Margaret House were preparing for A Levels and university Entrance: I gave classes, again unqualified, in English for non-native speakers. The boarding students slept in a separate adjoining house, and I was appointed the nun in charge of their nights. I slept in the kitchen downstairs on a camp bed, and washed in the very large sink.

It was a fulfilling life, but my focus on the life of the mind caught up with me. I read late into the night and even when forbidden to do so, I just could not stop. The Tudors and

Stuarts were fascinating and there was so much to discover and analyse. So it was decided I would not be allowed to take First Vows immediately on my return to Westgate: I would have to wait and prove my obedience. On my return to Westgate there was a new novice mistress: I was allowed to work in the scholasticate and wear the black veil, so humiliation was not public. Everyone in the community knew, of course. Sister Clare told me recently that she felt I resembled the gargoyle of St John the Baptist at Chartres Cathedral: thin and agonised. But six months later I took my First Vows, in the presence of the whole school at Mass.

7

Returning to Westgate after a year of the more collegiate life of Lady Margaret House, adjacent to Newnham College in Grange Road, Cambridge, it was surprisingly easy to come to terms with the externals of conventual life and to live in a world without carpets and with only wooden chairs, benches and stools. We were all Brides of Christ, enjoined to deny ourselves and to aim at perfection in the practice of virtue.

> They have left behind them all the riches of this world, their home, parents and family, their own will and liberty, their repose, ease and comfort, to let them sink as it were into oblivion. They have made themselves over to God wholeheartedly, and in spirit dwell now in heaven, for there is their coveted treasure, the sole object of their love and hope.

My failure in obedience, represented by the delay of my First Vows, motivated me even more strongly to concentrate on myself, to produce that conformity to God's will which I believed to be enshrined in the constitutions of the order and the voice of my superiors.

During these years faith became entirely subsumed into the surrender of self. Struggles and doubts I had, but not about theology or the Scriptures. The great dogmas of faith stood as it were like mountains on the skyline, fixed, immovable and true. The search seemed not for understanding, but for perfection in the outward details of a highly regulated life and for conquest in eliminating all personal desires and interests. Prayers were naturally offered for those outside the community, for the Church and the world: but the realities of existence were concentrated within the walls of the enclosure and above all in one's own mind. Despite our fundamental ignorance of each other, the community was all. Those who had left, whether of their own volition or by rejection, had their faces blacked out in any group photograph, and their names were never mentioned again. For those who remained, the aim was perfect obedience:

> They shall not argue as to whether the command be necessary or suitable, useful or opportune, still less shall they seek to probe the motives of their Superior . . . they must allow themselves to be shepherded or led like little children or innocent lambs who obey their shepherd even when he leads them straight to the slaughter.

I had been told that I must give up wanting to think and to read: my greatest contentment should be in manual labour, and in that I should be prepared to spend the rest of my days. But there was to be an intellectual renewal in the Catholic Church.

It was only the gradual impact of the Second Vatican Council that brought in glimpses of the thinking of the contemporary Church outside the convent. Now I find the words of many of the documents of Vatican II ponderous and massively opinionated; then they were heady with the assumption that debate was possible, that questions could be asked. The role of the Church in the modern world was being discussed: the static monolith of Counter-Reformation Catholicism, which I had known in 1950s Middlesbrough and in 1960s Kent, was being shaken, and challenging voices, some long frustrated, were being heard. In my order the results began to emerge strongly at the end of 1968 and in 1969. The externals of life changed rapidly: the religious habit was reformed, public penances were no more. More importantly it became possible to have access to books, to talk and to think.

For me these changes made a great difference. I continued to enjoy my teaching in the lower part of the secondary school and received great support especially from two of the lay teachers, Monica Cowell and Claire Sansom, who took me to evening lectures by the Workers' Educational Association. I was encouraged to study independently to prepare myself for university: I worked on Latin Advanced Level and Claire Sansom marked all my proses even during the school holidays. I was able to study the Scriptures and did two years of the Westminster Diploma of Theology in Scripture, Theology and Church History. In 1969 I sat the entrance examinations for Oxford and Cambridge, as was then allowed, and was accepted by Oxford. I thrilled to the theological investigations of Karl Rahner, joined in lively debates in anticipation of the long-awaited papal encyclical *Humanae Vitae*, considered the reform of religious life and the possibility of female priests and bishops.

For a time I enjoyed talking and listening and particularly being heard; the anxious young, with minds of their own, now seemed, even to superiors who had been in office for most of their adult lives and had demanded unquestioning obedience, the voice of the future and essential to the very survival of the order.

I became a *bonne ange* myself, to a delightfully questioning and strong-minded former pupil of Les Oiseaux. Fascinating speakers came to talk to the community: one, the distinguished theologian and Dominican Fergus Kerr, remains as a key influence in my approach to thinking to this day. He transformed the practice of Confession into a personal spiritual dialogue. But somehow hope of real change seemed thin. In July 1968, Pope Paul VI's encyclical *Humanae Vitae* reaffirmed the Catholic Church's teaching on birth control and abortion. Once more women were to be instructed and obedience demanded. In my own life, I was told that I could take up my Oxford place, but I would not be able to live in college: I would be placed for the duration of my degree in the house of another order in Oxford.

I had to face the issues of my changing view of religious life and my own commitment to it. After five years, these were immensely challenging. Indeed as I write today, forty-eight years later, I find myself resisting the necessary analysis. Just recently I ordered a copy of a French history of the order of Canonesses of St Augustine; when it arrived, my first sight on opening the package was a picture of a canoness in the traditional habit. My immediate reaction was to turn the book upside down, because I could not bear to look at the pin that had to be so carefully fastened to secure the veil, let alone the full-length black dress. In the autumn of 1969, though, I was prepared to analyse my views critically and ruthlessly.

I came to the conclusion that religious life, despite its long history, was unnecessary, misguided and potentially damaging. Believers could naturally decide individually whether to live simply, or chastely; but why not in the world? To become an educator was an honourable and important service to society; but this too must be a matter of choice and circumstances. My greatest animosity was towards the concept of obedience to another human being. However modern the terminology might become, it still involved the subjection of the mind. I needed to talk to a trusted friend who shared my doubts.

Now that personal conversations were possible, I heard from Clare about her journey as a canoness. She described it for me recently:

It was my perception at that time, the early sixties, that families were quietly delighted when a daughter believed she was being called to the 'religious life' – not so mine! They were mostly horrified or thought I was at the very least misguided. One brother, John, maintained until he died, that he and God 'fell out' when I became a nun. The day I left home, all five siblings came with my parents to Glasgow airport to wave me off, most with tears in their eyes and with a priest friend asking if anyone had told me that I could come back home if I wanted to. I think I was too much in shock to have any clear thoughts on that at all!

I had trained as a teacher and was dedicated and certain that teaching was my vocation, so it was not surprising that I joined an order that was devoted to the education of girls. The early days were guided by a professed nun, a kindly woman whom I admired and looked to for support. I felt she knew how I was feeling and understood, until we met in the corridor between the school and the enclosure and she walked on past me with her eyes cast down, without a nod or a smile. I needed more human contact than that.

In the months that followed, I was consumed by doubts. I thought I didn't 'fit in' and was sure that all the others were holier than I was. I did feel confident in my teaching and was encouraged when this was observed by senior staff. Throughout this time I had a heavy heart, but one evening having locked up the chapel, I vowed (to myself) that I would stay as long as I believed God wanted me to be there.

The heaviness lifted when it was suggested I spend the third year, the Apostolic Year, at our house in Uganda. By the time I left for there, I had taken the habit, which signified a commitment and helped me to feel part of the order. I shall never forget when the door of the plane opened and I smelled Africa for the first time – a smell of dry grass. I was met by two of the Nabbingo Community, who took me down from Kampala airstrip on the edge of Lake Victoria. I found in the Trinity College Nabbingo Community a group that I was in the main able to fit into. There was humour and affection and there was a dedication to the 'girls', whose ages ranged from early teens to early twenties, depending on when their families had enough coffee beans to cover the fees. They teased me and took advantage of my innocence and ignorance, but I was so pleased to be there that I took it, and both sides acknowledged that we were miles apart in our experience. A typical occasion was during a Saturday morning maths lesson, when it started to rain and all thirty of the girls scraped their chairs on the concrete floor and ran out, leaving me standing alone. They had gone to collect their washing, which was spread on various bushes to dry! I stood with my mouth wide open. I didn't even know they did their own laundry!

A year goes quickly and I suddenly found myself on a Raptim plane back to the UK. I thought my heart would break when I came home in a cold wet July to prepare for my first vows. Once again my family gathered to celebrate and support me as I moved on to the next stage of my life. After the ceremony, my mother made her way to my side and said it was so good to see me 'settled'. Some years later she told me I had said not a word in reply!

On returning to the novitiate, I discovered some changes, a few of them important ones. We were permitted to speak to each other in certain rooms and in particular in a little sitting room for the Professed. The movements effected by the Second Vatican Council were beginning to make an impact in the wider order.

There were discussions at all levels about how the order should be moving, and at a national gathering it was decided that there should be representatives of each level at a European meeting to be held in France.

These representatives were to be elected. Among those elected to this conference were Sr Judith (formerly Sr St Ann) and Sr Clare (formerly Sr St Benedict). Someone, probably Mother Vicar, decided that Sr Judith would be much too busy to attend and so others were elected. The order in France was much more forward looking than us, so it was an interesting conference. The younger sisters in the novitiate were worried by the ideas coming forward, expressed by John XXIIIs 'open all the windows and let the Spirit blow through'. Judith, on the other hand, was keen to hear all the ideas coming from France and so she and I often found ourselves in the little sitting room discussing where the order might go in the future.

Thus Clare and I began confidential conversations about our positions and our futures. We agreed that the changes that to us were essential would not come about and that our lives as canonesses would continue to be stressful and probably untenable. Final Vows were out of the question. We now felt it was not only difficult but irrelevant to try to up-date the vows of poverty, chastity and obedience, especially the last. Education was a different matter, but neither of us needed a vow: our commitment would last forever, but we needed personally to shape its development. I said in Confession, to a local priest, that my great sin was a desire to reform the Church: he told me it was no sin and I must continue, as fundamental change was essential. But I did not want to spend my energies, intellectual and practical in reconstructing with others a small and esoteric world that I now felt had no place for me. The choice of religious life had been the consequence of faith, but of a faith envisaged as complete and unshifting. Now it was my faith itself that needed to be explored and examined by the real and richly human methods of reading and thinking and talking. The search was on, and I was inspired by it. Once I had taken this intellectual step, the trappings of leaving religious life, seemingly so huge, were merely immediate and practical. There was no question now of blacking out faces and the ritual oblivion of departed nuns, but no amount of persuasion could induce me to remain in what I saw as a deeply-flawed society.

Clare agreed and we informed the Mother Superior. We were obliged stay for two terms until the end of the academic session, not because of the end of our First Vows but because we were teaching in the school and caring for its boarders. It was a long six months and we needed the strength of our friendship and the openness of our discourse with each other, in private, to see us through. Clare's parish priest visited her from Glasgow and asked if there was anything that would help us. She immediately suggested 100 cigarettes and he promptly obliged, with the utmost discretion. So each evening, once the boarders and the nuns were asleep, we crept out by an unlocked back door and sat on a tree trunk in the garden, with one cigarette each and much to confide. It worked, until that uplifting July morning when we caught our train to London.

So there were the years of the smart A5 notebooks that I destroyed without regret. There was no pause in my life. Somehow I sloughed off not simply the details of the nun's daily round, but the more debased of the habits of mind of those six years. But that is not to say that their influence has not been profound. Never again could I regard the tenets of faith as given, timeless or unchanging. Every phrase in a credal formulation is for me a matter of historical context and lively debate. I am suspicious of closed institutions, of self-important hierarchies, of clerical superiority. I cannot be told what to believe, and I find it difficult to accept the advice or the insights of a preacher who makes assumptions about the faith of his or her congregation. Faith is a huge baggy monster for me; it is not coherent and ordered and it is in constant need of exploration. The scriptures are there to be read and examined and understood, as each part was written in its own historical context, as it has been interpreted in different societies, and as it is understood now. Above all the mind is there to be free and to be used, and never to be dominated. I understand now, as I never did at grammar school in my first Latin lessons, why *anima*, like its Greek and Hebrew counterparts, means 'mind', 'soul' and 'spirit'. Since I gave up trying to deny my own integrity, I have known all three to be one. My faith and my life have been in a constant state of tension, but never so much and with such effects as during those six years between 1964 and 1970. What has endured from my early years, and will forever, are love, learning and education. Snowflakes do indeed descend in all directions.